THE LAND OF STEVIN AND HUYGENS

STUDIES IN THE HISTORY
OF MODERN SCIENCE

Editors:

ROBERT S. COHEN, *Boston University*

ERWIN N. HIEBERT, *Harvard University*

EVERETT I. MENDELSOHN, *Harvard University*

VOLUME 7

DIRK J. STRUIK

Professor of Mathematics, Emeritus, M.I.T.

THE LAND OF
STEVIN AND HUYGENS

*A Sketch of Science and Technology
in the Dutch Republic during the Golden Century*

D. REIDEL PUBLISHING COMPANY

DORDRECHT : HOLLAND / BOSTON : U.S.A.

LONDON : ENGLAND

Library of Congress Cataloging in Publication Data

Struik, Dirk Jan, 1894–
    The land of Stevin and Huygens.

    (Studies in the history of modern science ; v. 7)
    Translation of: Het land van Stevin en Huygens. With corrections and
additional material.
    Bibliography: p.
    Includes indexes.
        1. Science—Netherlands—History. 2. Stevin, Simon, 1548–1620.
3. Huygens, Christiaan, 1629–1695. I. Title. II. Series.
Q127.N2S713   509'.492   81–1848
ISBN 90–277–1236–0   AACR2
ISBN 90–277–1237–9 (pbk.)

Published by D. Reidel Publishing Company,
P.O. Box 17, 3300 AA Dordrecht, Holland.

Sold and distributed in the U.S.A. and Canada
by Kluwer Boston Inc.
190 Old Derby Street, Hingham, MA 02043, U.S.A.

In all other countries, sold and distributed
by Kluwer Academic Publishers Group,
P.O. Box 322, 3300 AH Dordrecht, Holland.

D. Reidel Publishing Company is a member of the Kluwer Group.

Printed in The Netherlands

*Dedicated to
the memory of
Anton Struik*

TABLE OF CONTENTS

LIST OF ILLUSTRATIONS

(Between pages 28 and 29)

Willem Bleau's globe
A Flemish astrolabe made by Michael Coignet
Title page of Vesalius's *De humani corporis fabrica* (1543)
Petrus Planicus at age seventy (1622)
Lecture on navigation by the Reverend P. Planicus
Map of the Polar Region, from Linschoten
Willebrord Snellius
Jan Adriaansz. Leeghwater

(Between pages 76 and 77)

Simon Stevin
Title page of *The Art of Weighing* by Stevin
Paper mill at the Open Air Museum, Arnhem
Water mill at Wijk-bij-Duurstede
Réné Descartes
Frans van Schooten Junior
Christiaan Huygens
The "Hofwijck" near The Hague

(*Between pages 124 and 125*)

INTRODUCTION TO THE ENGLISH EDITION

During the later Middle Ages, the Low Countries, or Netherlands, were divided into a number of feudal principalities headed by such lords as the counts of Holland, the counts of Flanders, the counts, later dukes, of Gelderland (Guelders), the dukes of Brabant and of Hainaut and the bishop of Utrecht. The principalities were known as the seventeen Netherlands. During the fifteenth century most of them became part of the domain of the dukes of Burgundy with their splendid court at Brussels. These dukes began a system of centralization, continued with some success by their successors of the House of Habsburg. It was the Habsburg emperor Charles V who, in 1543, succeeded in incorporating all seventeen Netherlands as provinces of his vast empire, extending from America to Spain, Austria, Germany and the Netherlands.

This was the time of the Reformation which came to the Netherlands first as Lutheranism, then as Calvinism. The persecutions, together with attempted inroads into the jealously guarded rights and privileges of towns and provinces by the Brussels administration, fostered feelings of resentment. This lead to actual rebellion in the days of Philip II, Charles' son and successor, who tried to rule from Spain and to enforce the Catholic religion much more strictly than his father. In 1567, he sent the duke of Alva with an army to the Netherlands. Armed resistance began in 1568, opening the Eighty Year War. At first Alva could book some successes, but the tide turned on the first of April, 1572 (a date remembered in the Northern Netherlands like the nineteenth of April, 1775, in the U.S.A.) with the capture of the town of Den Briel in Holland by rebellious anti-Catholic pirates (called *Geuzen* after the French *gueux*, beggars). Many towns now shook off what was felt as the Spanish yoke. Alva's counter-offensive, consisting of a series of sieges, was at first successful, but met defeat at the walls of Alkmaar (1573) and Leiden (1574). The Spanish had more success in the Southern Provinces, a success culminating in the recapture of Antwerp (1585). In 1579 the Northern Provinces had already built a loose federation in the Union of Utrecht, resulting in what became known as the Union of the Seven Provinces (Holland, Zeeland, Utrecht, Gelderland, Overysel, Friesland, Groningen plus the territory of Drente). The leading genius was William of Orange, *dit* William the Silent, probably on account of his diplomatic tact. The Southern Provinces eventually returned to Spain and the Catholic Church. The Northern Union, often called the Dutch Republic, was dominated by the Calvinists, organized in the Reformed Church, although a large number of its inhabitants remained faithful to Catholicism.

The formal abjuration of Philip II by the North occurred in 1581. William the Silent was assassinated in 1584, but the war against Spain continued successfully under the strategic leadership of his son Maurice, and, after his death in 1625, of his brother Frederic Henry (the grandfather of William III, king of England). These princes bore the title of *stadhouder* (lit.: lieutenant). The constitutional structure of the Republic and the creation of its powerful position in the world was the work of the jurist-statesman Johan van Oldenbarnevelt.

There was a truce from 1609 to 1621, troubled by the religious conflict between Remonstrants or Arminians, representing in the main patrician merchants with a section of the more liberal intellectuals – one of the most famous being Hugo Grotius – and the Counter-Remonstrants, orthodox Calvinists with their strength in the popular masses led by their preachers and supported after 1617 by Maurice. This struggle led to the execution of van Oldenbarnevelt (1619). Despite a temporary victory of the Counter-

Remonstrants, the Republic continued to be ruled by a dominant section of the merchant patriciate, the so-called Regents (*Regenten*), of whom those at the head of Amsterdam were the most powerful. They exercised their power, usually successfully, through the States General meeting at The Hague, composed of delegates sent by the States of the provinces, among whom the States of Holland were again the most influential.

The official religion was Dutch Reformed (Calvinist), but other Protestant sects, Lutherans, Baptists, Collegiants and others, were usually not molested. Neither were the Jews, concentrated in Amsterdam, and as a rule even the Catholics could meet, but supposedly in secret ("Our dear Lord in the attic", a hidden Catholic church in Amsterdam, now a tourist attraction).

Peace with Spain came in 1648 with the peace of Westphalia. The Republic emerged as a major power in the Atlantic world. In art we speak of this period in its existence as the age of Rembrandt. In science, as we hope to show, we may likewise speak of the age of Stevin and Huygens.

*   *   *   *   *

From what has been sketched above it will be clear that the word Holland in this book is not used, as so often in the present, for what is now the kingdom of the Netherlands. Holland, for us and in accordance with history, is a territory, first county, then province, in the Western region of the Low Countries near the North Sea. It is the richest part of the North; in it are many of the leading cities, such as Hoorn, Enkhuizen, Alkmaar, Amsterdam, Haarlem, Delft, Rotterdam, Dordrecht as well as The Hague, the center of government of the Republic. This Holland has been, since 1840, divided into the two present provinces North and South Holland.

The Southern Netherlands have been called Belgium from time to time in this book, because its territory is essentially that of the present kingdom with that name, established in 1830. Before that time they belonged first to Spain, then to Austria and then to the United Kingdom of the Netherlands, founded in 1815 and split in two by the revolution of 1830.

The word 'Dutch', derived from an ancient Germanic word meaning people, will be used for the language as well as the people of the Northern Netherlands.

*   *   *   *   *

The translation from the original Dutch edition (1958, revised ed. 1979) is by the author, who takes all responsibility for the text. This text, though at most places a direct translation from the original, has been amended at places by some corrections and additional material, as in the last chapter on colonial science. In the translation I have been assisted by Mrs. Renate Hanauer and by Dr. Ruth Struik and have been encouraged by Professors Robert S. Cohen of Boston University and Erwin N. Hiebert of Harvard University. To all these friends I express my appreciation for their assistance.

PREFACE TO THE FIRST DUTCH EDITION

What we usually call the Golden Age or Golden Century of the Netherlands starts around 1580–1590 with the earlier years of the Republic and comes to an end with the last years of the seventeenth century. We know it as the time of Oldenbarnevelt and De Witt, the time of the great princes of the House of Orange, the time of the admirals Tromp and De Ruyter, the time of Frans Hals and Rembrandt. It is also a period of important contributions to science, and in this respect may be characterized by the names of Stevin and Huygens, the representative figures at the beginning and the end of the period. Compared to what has been written about the politics, the art of warfare and the arts in general of the Golden Century, the literature on the science (and technology) of the period is of very modest dimensions. There exists a small number of special studies about certain definite persons and fields of science, supplemented by the monumental edition of the works of Huygens and by equally valuable editions of the works of Beeckman, Stevin and van Leeuwenhoek. But there exists, as far as I know, no book that attempts to give an overall picture of the whole scientific development. This is a pity, not only because the image of the Golden Century is distorted in this way, but also because Dutch science of this period is so rich. In the small world of Amsterdam and surrounding cities representatives could be found of almost all sciences cultivated at that time; moreover, many of these representatives were leaders in their field, be it the study of mathematics, mechanics or physics, chemistry, biology or medicine, the work with map, telescope or microscope. The history of science in the Republic is a good introduction to the history of the formative years of our present-day science in general.

What we offer here is not such a book. For this we need more study of sources than is possible in a domain so little explored as Dutch science in the Golden Age. But we hope that our survey can give a not too inadequate picture of the different forms of science and technology cultivated in those interesting years. Such a picture may show the importance of this development and introduce to a more general public some of the principal actors. They certainly merit our attention, these gentlemen called Waghenaer, Plancius, Stevin, Beeckman, van Schooten, Huygens, Tulp, Ruysch, Swammerdam, van Leeuwenhoek and so many others, among whom such better known men as De Witt, Descartes and Maurice of Orange stand out in their own way, but presented here in a somewhat different light.

We believe that the work of these men can be better understood, if it is sketched against a background illuminated by facts from the economic, political, religious and general cultural life in the Republic.

We have only mentioned a minimum of sources; a book like this should not become top-heavy with footnote erudition. Those who look at the bibliography at the end usually can reach the primary sources without much trouble — and in the process discover many more interesting facts and persons than have been presented here in this book: the Golden Century was rich in interesting and picturesque figures. What a creative vitality existed in the Dutch people of those days! What a promise for the future when the whole Dutch people will have a chance to develop its creative powers!

Let us end with a remark made by an older contemporary of Huygens and Newton, a naturalist in his own way, and, if not the most learned of the ichthyologists, then certainly the most pleasant one:

I might say more, but it is not fit for this
place; but if this Discourse which follows
shall come to a second impression, which is
possible for slight books have been in this
Age observed to have that fortune; I shall
then for thy sake be glad to correct what is
faulty, or by a conference with any to
explain or enlarge what is defective: but
for this time I have neither a willingness
nor leisure to say more than wish thee a
rainy evening to read this book in.
Farewell.

From: Izaak Walton, *The Compleat Angler*, 1653.

Belmont, Massachusetts
28 November 1957

PREFACE TO THE THIRD, REVISED DUTCH EDITION

The famous angler quoted in my first preface had the hope that his little book might at some time come to a second edition. His hope has been more than fulfilled. But the time has also come that this little book on the land of Stevin and Huygens and so many other excellent scientists will be reprinted. Here, therefore, is the opportunity to, quoting once more the good Walton, "correct what is faulty, or . . . to explain or enlarge what is defective." These corrections and enlargements are found in the text and in the notes; I have used the opportunity to introduce certain persons such as Dapper and Glauber whom I had not mentioned before and to give a little more information about certain other personalities such as Blasius and Hartsoecker.

The book has remained quite short and we still look forward to a solid book or to more solid books in which the remarkable scientific (and technological) achievements and results of the Dutch Golden Century will at last be described and interpreted. Is the time not more than overdue that, with all the attention given to the political, military, literary and artistic life of the Republic, more attention be paid to the important role played by the Republic in the Golden Century and long after in the scientific life of Europe? And not only science, but also technology: the wind and water mills, the drainage of lakes and construction of dikes, the military and hydraulic engineering in the Republic were well developed and often exemplary for their period. It seems that the history of science and technology still remains, after the word of Dijksterhuis, Clio's stepchild.

I am glad to say that the muse of history has not been so partial in the domain of special investigations. We have the editions of the collected works (or an important part of them) of Stevin, Huygens and van Leeuwenhoek and an increasing number of monographs in books and periodicals dealing with mathematics, physics, chemistry, biology, medicine and technology. The philosophical background characterized by the gradual transition from an orthodox, modified Aristotelianism to Cartesianism and its further developments, often critical, also attracts a growing number of students and has found a comprehensive treatment in the book of the late Professor Sassen.

I have somewhat extended the bibliography of the first edition.

Belmont, Massachusetts
12 June 1978

CHAPTER I

THE YOUNG REPUBLIC

The rise and growth of the Dutch Republic[1] will always fill us with amazement and a desire for understanding. Here was a people of artisans, shopkeepers, sailors and merchants that defeated the best armies of Europe, had created a land of industrious and growing cities, with a mighty fleet and an excellent transportation system, a flourishing agriculture and horticulture, an exemplary financial condition, a country that created poets, artists, scholars, engineers and scientists and created an art which in its way has never been surpassed. Natives and strangers were impressed. "How is it done?" they asked abroad. An Englishman who, in 1614, witnessed the departure of the herring fleet from Amsterdam, a fleet of a thousand sail, exclaimed that "no king on earth has ever seen a fleet such as this being equipped by his subjects." The French Duke De Rohan, visiting Amsterdam in 1600, said that nobody could believe it who had not seen it, but there were from three to four thousand sailing vessels on the quays, twice a year fleets of between four hundred and five hundred ships arrived with wheat from Danzig, wine and salt from France and Spain and, moreover, other ships laden with spices and other precious commodities from India and the newly discovered countries. It was especially hard on the English, who themselves were busy creating a commercial empire, not to speak of the Spanish and Portuguese. Queen Elizabeth had to hear that Holland and Zeeland alone possessed more ships and ship's mates than her whole country and that every year almost a thousand new ships were being constructed. True, all this prosperity was accompanied by much misery, equally true that this prosperity was actually based on this

1

misery, but this was only too often seen as a natural phenomenon, ordained by God. The fact remains that thousands of families in Hoorn, Enkhuizen, Amsterdam, Rotterdam, Dordrecht, Flushing and other mercantile towns were helped to their bread by maritime and inland trade and often helped to more than bread alone. English statesmen and economists from Sir Walter Raleigh under Elizabeth to William Petty under Charles II persisted in investigating the Dutch phenomenon and keeping it before the eyes of their countrymen. For the mentality of seventeenth century Europe the Republic seemed to be a kind of model community.

Not only commerce and fleet led to admiration and envy. The drainages in Holland and Zeeland inspired the English kings James I and Charles I to reclaim the East Anglian swamps under the supervision of the engineer Vermuyden from Zeeland. Dutch sea and country maps from the houses of Hondius and Blaeu were considered the best and most beautiful on earth. Who could publish more attractive books than Elzevier and Plantin? Who had ever travelled in a more pleasant way than on a Dutch towboat, gliding on the canals through a prosperous landscape with gardens, meadows and cattle? Where was a better military training school than the Army of the States under the Princes of Orange? Which university had greater scholars than Leiden? Even Newton did not deem it beneath his dignity to prepare in England a Latin translation of the *Algebra* of the now forgotten Kinckhuyzen.[2]

What was the secret of this prosperity and this influence? The faithful invoked the Deity — as the Psalmist says: "Blessed be the Lord God of Israel, who only doeth wondrous things" — or they invoked the memory of William the Silent who already, at the beginning of the rebellion, had concluded a solid covenant "with the supreme Potentate of all Potentates." Others looked for more secular explanations. William Petty, the well-known English economist, presented in his *Political Arithmetic* of 1677 a whole series of such causes from the fertility of the soil to the freedom of conscience and the confidence in the legal system. To us two factors come easily to mind. The Northern Netherlands, as they developed during and after the Eighty Year War, were a pure burgher community, not weighed down by the burden of feudal authorities such as kings, knights, barons and junkers that ruled the roost in the neighboring countries until, at any rate in England, the Revolution of 1642–1649 under Cromwell put some obstacles in their way. The regent patricians might freely acquire letters of nobility and call themselves Lord of Sommelsdijk or Lord of Zuylichem, their power was based on money and not on land. And secondly, the Hollanders and the Zeelanders knew to use their old superiority in vessels and crew to all possible advantage, now that the heart of European commerce had been moved from the Mediterranean to the North Sea, and were able to maintain this exceptional position with respect to the surrounding countries for many years. We must also not forget that already from the time of the Middle Ages a general atmosphere of religious tolerance existed, at any rate among an important section of the population – we think of the figure of Erasmus and of the "Erasmian" attitude of leading merchants and intellectuals. This allowed the Dutch to deal freely with other peoples, even those across the oceans – and also attract those from other countries who saw themselves oppressed.

In Asia and America a whole new world was opened to merchant and sailor with prospects not only of gaining great profits, but also of singeing the beard of the Spanish king. Added to this was that under the Spanish persecutions many families from the South had emigrated to the North, families of enterprising, wealthy and well-informed merchants as well as humanists and experts in navigation, geography and other fields. The Republic had the men, the means, the power and the pluck. True, also the appropriate ideals and pre-judices: the Calvinist belief in a special covenant of grace with God – "the God of the Netherlands" – and a conviction that in the

making of profit God intended to bless a person; the class belief
of the "lords" that "het grauw" (the populace) existed to sweat
and, if necessary, to give its life for them and the almost national
belief that the "natives" of the overseas territories were created
not only to be dominated and exploited, but even, if necessary,
be exterminated if mercantile policy demanded it.

Before the war the mercantile marine was almost entirely of
a coastal nature, fisheries and trade with surrounding countries,
especially the Baltic regions, England, France, Spain, Portugal. The
liberation offered an opportunity to extend maritime expansion.
Difficulties placed in the way by the Iberian majesties, such as
prohibition of trade with the countries under their crown, were
conquered by extending this trade to the countries across the sea
themselves and by sailing through the Strait of Gibraltar into the
Mediterranean actually under the nose of the Spanish. A large
number of Dutchmen had experience in Spanish or Portuguese
service; the time had come to place this experience at the disposal
of their own country.

This was the beginning of the so-called *Grote Vaart* (Major Traffic) to Africa, India and America which yielded great treasures in
the seventeenth century. It eventually established through commerce, war and piracy, including the slave trade, the Dutch colonial
empire. Coastal traffic and fisheries continued to flourish and so
did the transit traffic. Amsterdam became the great mercantile
city which, to quote the poet Vondel, "unfolding itself majesti-
cally on the rivers Amstel and Y carried as empress the crown of
Europe".[3] The Hague became an important diplomatic center.
And in all these industrial and commercial towns lived and worked
in houses large and small with step gables, stoops and *luifels*[4]
the owners of these fleets and their skippers, the instructors in
navigation and arithmetic, the designers of charts and instruments
that made the dangerous sea traffic as safe as possible with the
most modern precautions. Here we find also physicians, surveyors,

printers, students of living and lifeless nature, also common and Latin schools, and from 1575 on in Leiden a university, followed before the end of the century by one in Franeker in Frisia and by others in the next century.

We see, therefore, that there was interest in and stimulation for the cultivation of science and the opportunity to bring this science into practice. Let us have a look at the nature of this science.

CHAPTER II

ANCIENT SCIENCE

1

The rise of the Republic took place in the same century in which science in Europe began to escape for the first time from the framework of the traditional Asian-Greek outlook on the world. This sixteenth century development was the forerunner of that enormous revolution in the intellectual life of the next century connected with the names of Galileo, Descartes, Huygens and Newton. The Republic with its particular type of civic institutions, its wealth and its courage was one of the countries in which both this preparation as well as this revolution itself could take place. This makes the study of the sciences in the Golden Century so attractive and instructive: in that seemingly so narrow world of Amsterdam and the surrounding towns the great events of the world were reflected and activated.

For thousands of years Asia had been the leader in the cultivation of the mathematical, physical and medical sciences as well as in technology. Sometimes China was leading, then again India or Mesopotamia or Egypt — since we can associate Egypt in many respects with the cultural domain of Asia. Knowledge was exchanged along the caravan routes and along the seas to be assimilated or rejected according to the ways of the land. In all these centuries there had been only one important exception to the general cultural pattern, and that was the marvelous period of Greek civilization. The creative period of this civilization only lasted a few centuries, but in these centuries it created undying scientific, literary and philosophical values. Asia marveled at this miraculous flowering and, for so far as it affected its scientific traditions, tried to assimilate the new ideas, not without difficulties, however, since the rational methods of Greek thought were often in conflict with the traditional religious concepts prevailing in the ancient cultures. Added to it was the fact that with Alexander the Great, Greek civilization came to the East as the heritage of conquerors and usurpers and this often brought political as well as emotional elements into the conflict. This was especially strong in Egypt and West Asia, countries with the closest contact with the Greek world. With the coming of Islam this contact was broken politically, but the exchange of scientific ideas continued. Greek mathematics and astronomy as well as medicine were made available in Arabic, and the Hindu-Arabic numbers with the ten symbols 0, 1, 2 ... 9 gradually moved westward. Generally speaking, the traditional routes remained open.

After the tenth century the feudal system in Europe began to establish itself and towns appeared, at the beginning, entirely inside the confines of the system. Some cities developed into powerful commerical centers that began to reject the tyranny of the feudal lords. Their prosperity was derived to a great extent from the trade with Asia and its silk, spices, jewelry and other precious commodities. Constantinople also played an important role. With the stream of commodities came science and technology, first to Italy and from there to Spain, France, Germany, England, the Netherlands and other countries of Europe. Where Arabic was the general scholarly language of the Islamic world, Greek that of Constantinople and the East Roman empire, Latin was that of the world of the Roman Catholic Christians. Many manuscripts were, therefore, translated in the twelfth and thirteenth centuries from Arabic into Latin, sometimes also from the Greek, Syriac and Hebrew. When, in the fourteenth and fifteenth centuries, European feudalism began to decay, this scientific interest increased considerably because the decline of the landed lords was narrowly related to the growth of the commercial cities. The local market was replaced by the general commodity market, the narrow feudal relationships by money economy. The commercial cities were flowering, merchants became bankers, money became the driving power commanding townsman and knight, emperor and Pope. And in the magnificence of Papal and princely courts, in the palaces of the great merchants and bankers there was interest in the Greek classics, and new works of art and science were created. This was the Renaissance period, accompanied by the revival of classical studies known as Humanism. The most famous Dutch humanist was Erasmus, who published among many other writings the Greek text of the New Testament (1516) with a Latin translation. It was this Erasmus edition that Luther used for his German bible translation.

This period also witnessed the attempts to obtain the treasures of Asia independently of the old caravan routes. Under the direction, first of the Portuguese, then of the Spanish, great voyages of discovery were undertaken on the ocean alongside of Africa and further to India and China to the East, as well as across the ocean to the West. A by-product was the discovery of an entirely new part of the world that would also be forced to send its treasures to the European rulers. The name of this new continent, America, reminds us of the financial powers that were intimately connected with this enormous expansion; Amerigo Vespucci [1] was a humanist related to the Florentine commercial and banking house of the Medici.

This extension of commerce and the circulation of precious metals stimulated again the money economy and with it the power and the self-confidence of the European merchants and of the princes and feudal lords with sufficient credit to carry on a big household. Here and there we see already merchant and banker occupied with manufacture and mining and in this way involved in a budding capitalist form of economy. Such ruling classes with their learned men and artists were not satisfied to entertain themselves simply in the framework of a traditional culture, how endowed it may have been with certain admirable traits. The number of inventions was increasing, several taken over from Asia such as the compass, gun powder, printing, different technical procedures in the production of glass, textiles, steel and other fields, as well as wind and water mills, and improvements continued. The time had come to surpass the Greek-Arabic world also in the sciences.

2

Let us give a short summary of this traditional Greek-Arabic science. The general world picture was derived from the Greek philosopher Aristotle whose work in the twelfth and thirteenth centuries had been brought into harmony with the Islamic religion by Averroës,[2] with the Jewish religion by Maimonides[3] and by Thomas Aquinas[4] with the Catholic religion. It is not difficult for us to appreciate Greek sculpture, Arabic architecture or Jewish Scripture. This is the more remarkable when we realize how difficult it is for us to see the world, especially nature, through Aristotelian eyes. Our present concepts of nature, originating in the seventeenth century, have become so familiar to us through school and life that in many respects we feel alien to the medieval philosophy of nature – with the possible exception of some Thomistically educated priests. In this Aristotelian world picture objects and actions in nature were determined not so much by "quantity" as by "quality", so that there was little interest in the "how much"; experiment played hardly any role; the earth was fixed and subjected to other laws than the world of the stars; it was difficult to bring these laws into a precise mathematical form and this did not even occur to most scientifically inclined philosophers. Terrestrial objects were combinations of the four elements fire, air, earth and water. Here qualities came into the picture. Where we think in such terms as specific gravity and calories, Aristotle thought in such concepts as dry and humid, warm and cold, so that the earth was dry and cold, water cold and humid, the air humid and warm and fire warm and dry, and very few people brought some degree of measurement to these concepts. We also miss in the Aristotelian model such measurable concepts as mass, force, energy, moments (except in the most elementary cases). We do meet such concepts as substance and form, potential and actual. Aristotle defined for instance motion as transition from the potential to the actual, a way of thinking not really wrong, but it does not tell us how we can measure motion. He distinguished between four causes, usually indicated by their Latin names: *causa materialis* or material cause, *causa formalis* or formal cause, *causa efficiens* or efficient cause, *causa finalis* or final cause. If we construct a chair, then wood is the material cause, the work of the carpenter the efficient cause, the shape of the chair the formal cause and the activity of sitting the final cause. This all makes us impatient, because it represents a way of life with a simple technology and uncomplicated relations between human beings: when we want to understand the telephone, we do not inquire so much into all the different *causae*, but study the laws of Maxwell and Kirchhoff, hence the efficient cause. The final cause which plays such an important role with Aristotle has been pushed into the background in our modern theories about physics and chemistry. (Not quite. Can computers set themselves a goal?) Aristotle, furthermore, considered the earth as a sphere fixed in space, surrounded by spheres in which moon, sun, planets and other stars were moving. In the "sublunary" world, hence on earth, every element had its "natural" place; earth and water "tend" toward the center of the earth; they had "gravity". Light and fire "tend" to get away from it. They had "levity". The natural motion of a composite body is determined by the interaction of all these tendencies. However, there also exist forced, unnatural, motions as for instance that of a stone being thrown. Every such motion, therefore, must have a "mover" or in a famous Latin sentence: *Omne quod movetur ab alio movetur*, everything that moves is moved by something else. The mover may be inside the moved object as the soul in a living body, but also outside of it, but then it must be in immediate contact. Action at a distance is unthinkable to Aristotle. According to this theory something has to push an object that has been thrown away as a pushcart by a hawker (we see again how narrowly the Aristotelian ideas reflect the period of simple crafts). Aristotle sees this "something" in the action of the medium, e.g., the air. The velocity of a body is then proportional to the moving force and inversely proportional to the resistance of the medium. But do not believe that these concepts of force and velocity are precisely defined. Aristotle could do this only for uniform velocities. In the later Middle Ages, when the development of trade and craft led even some Scholastic philosophers more and more into a more quantitative outlook, there were heroic attempts also to define precisely uniform accelerations and even something like the concept of inertia. And if an object would fall in a vacuum with resistance zero, such an object would have infinite velocity, and since this is unthinkable, Aristotle concludes that there is no vacuum.

All this is valid for the sublunary world. In the world of the stars the situation is quite different. There we do not have only the four elements, but a fifth one, the substance of the stars, the *quinta essentia* (quintessence). The earth is fixed because there is nothing in the four elements that can lead to a rotation. The motion of the celestial spheres is therefore a true rotation. The natural motion of all that consists of *quinta essentia* is, therefore, circular. Outside of the celestial spheres, where the Christians placed the Deity, is the origin of the motion, the *Prima Movens* — "l'Amor que muove il sole e l'altre stelle", "the Love that moves the sun and the other stars" in the words of Dante. Whoever will understand Dante's *Divina Commedia* has to understand something of the Aristotelian model of the world.

3

This was all very beautiful and consistent, but the only thing you could do with it was to speculate a little more. Astronomers, pilots, instrument makers, engineers, teachers of counting and surveying derived little advantage from Aristotle, and these were exactly the men who began to take a prominent place in the early capitalist period. No wonder that many men who in the sixteenth century advanced the natural sciences had little or nothing to do with the universities or only with such universities as that of Padua where under the aegis of the Venetian commercial aristocracy there had for a long time been a critical attitude to Aristotle. All this speculation or babbling, as they began to say in the sixteenth century (just read a few chapters in Erasmus' *Praise of Folly*), should not make us forget that Aristotle's natural history is in many respects far better than his mechanics. He was an excellent observer who apparently liked to talk with "ordinary" people such as fishermen, farmers or hunters, and in some of his observations on animals, especially fish, he was so far in advance of his time that he has only been vindicated in the nineteenth century.[5] It seems that he even experimented himself, dissected animals but probably not human beings. Indeed, if we compare Aristotle's clever, but to us often idle speculation on inanimate nature, with his equally clever, but often correct observations in the realm of living beings, we might describe him as a biologist gone amiss. This, however, is a remark that takes no account of the socio-economic conditions under which Aristotle worked and is therefore entirely unhistorical. But even Aristotle's theory of nature and his philosophy have never lost all vital substance; his logic has always been

taken seriously and forms the foundation of our modern mathematical logic. The Catholic Church has never broken entirely with
Aristotle and has a preference for his philosophy in the Christian
framework created by Thomas Aquinas. There is a good deal of
Thomism in Catholic lecture courses and there we can still find a
serious discussion of the *Omne quod movet ab alio movetur*.

In antique medicine we also find those mixed elements of pure
observation and speculation. The so-called Hippocratic corpus,
containing about sixty medical essays, was well known to the humanists. These essays, written under the influence of Hippocrates
of Cos, an older contemporary of Plato, contain a great number of
descriptions of practical cases, indicating to the physician the
method he should follow. Another authority was the Greek physician Galen of Pergamon, of the second century of our era, who
resided for many years in Rome and wrote his many works under
Hippocratic and Aristotelian-Platonic influence. His system was
until the seventeenth century the accepted basis for the physiology
of the body. In accordance with the doctrine of the four elements,
Galen accepted four elementary qualities in the body, the *humores*:
blood (*sanguis*), slime (*phlegma*) black bile (*melan cholè*), and
yellow bile (*cholè*); on their distribution in the body depended
health, sickness and the human condition in general. We still
speak of sanguine, phlegmatic, melancholic and choleric tempers.
With these humors special organs in the body were connected.
The heart was the organ of heat and also maintained a kind of
oscillating motion of the blood. This blood was obtained in the
liver from the food, sent to the heart ventricles and used for the
further maintenance of the body. Galen dissected animals, but
no human beings. What he knew of human beings he derived from
the dissection of animals, especially of the Barbary ape, probably
that animal, *Macaca sylvana*, so long popular as a Gibraltar tourist
attraction. There was a vital principle, the spirits or pneuma, obtained through breathing that brought that spirit into lung and

left heart ventricle where it got into contact with the blood by a supposed connection of left and right ventricle. We still speak of vital spirits; the influence of Galen can still be felt in our language, even if his physiology can no longer be accepted. But the humanists also knew other medical authorities, among them the Arabic-writing Persian philosopher Ibn Sinā of the eleventh century known by the Latin name of Avicenna, whose "Canon of Medicine" was perhaps held in even higher esteem than the works of Galen. It has long remained supreme in Islam, where he has often been called the Prince of all learning.

The practical astronomers belonged to those people who could not find much use in the qualitative theories of Aristotle. They had to deal with measurable things, observations. Here they were helped by the theory of Ptolemy, explained in his astronomical treatise known as the *Almagest*, a curious semi-Arabic, semi-Greek title. Here could be found a thoroughly mathematical theory of the motion of the sun, moon and planets that enabled astronomers to give an account of the position of these celestial bodies with considerable precision and to forecast eclipses, conjunctions and oppositions. The disadvantage was that Ptolemy, whose celestial bodies moved in circles on circles in so-called epicycloids around a fixed spherical earth, could not give a physical explanation of his system; Aristotle, to the contrary, had his celestial system solidly anchored in his whole philosophy of nature. This left the practical astronomers rather cold, so long as the Ptolemaic theory could give the correct answers or, to use the standing phrase, "save the phenomena" — an early example of a form of positivism without elevating it to the rank of a philosophy. This kind of dualism, a satisfying mathematical system without a good physical underpinning and a satisfying physics without mathematical support, was unsolvable during the Middle Ages, and the Scholastics could only hope that at some time or other the Divine Wisdom would offer a way out. And indeed, the Divine Wisdom has actually done this very thing, but in a much more radical way than the learned minds ever expected: by providing a European revolution during which both Ptolemy and Aristotle would be toppled from their thrones.

Ptolemy had also written a book on geography that only became known in Europe during the fifteenth century. It taught how to determine places on earth by latitude and longitude and how the earth could be mapped on a plane with mathematical accuracy. This *Geographia* marks the beginning of scientific geography in Europe and accomplished this exactly in a period where voyages of discovery made this knowledge more than ever necessary. It was a pity that Ptolemy's acquaintance with the earth left much to be desired, even in the Mediterranean regions where Ptolemy was at home. This sea itself was represented as much too large: it stretches in the *Geographia* over sixty degrees of longitude where in reality there are only forty, yet Ptolemy's geography was a great step forward if compared with the old-fashioned scholastic map conceptions in which neither latitude nor longitude played a role. There also existed so-called *portolani* maps for the practical use of sailors based on empirical knowledge and in some respects quite accurate though composed without any mathematical theory. These maps, where sailing directions were represented by straight lines based on compass directions, existed almost exclusively for the Mediterranean and its coasts.

The teachers of arithmetic and the merchants used to count with the so-called abacus, a kind of counting frame, writing down the results in Roman numerals, but towards the end of the Middle Ages the so-called Hindu-Arabic decimal position system came into use. This system is nothing but our present mode of counting with the ten symbols of 0, 1, 2 ... 9 and a rule that, say, an "8" on the third position to the left in 813 means 800. This system was a great improvement and the triumphs of arithmetic in the sixteenth century would have been impossible without this invention.

Algebra, which already in its name shows how it had been developed and transmitted by writers using the Arabic language, consisted mainly in the art of solving equations of the first and second degree. It did not really come to any significant improvement in Europe till Renaissance days, a period witnessing also the development of trigonometry, a science half of Arabic, half of Ptolemaic origin. Geometry was studied primarily from the *Elements* of Euclid, if only in less rigorous form,[6] often as a basis for mensuration. These *Elements*, composed around 300 B.C. in Egypt, formed a textbook for the study of plane and solid geometry as well as for theoretical arithmetic. This book in which theorems are derived by logical reasoning from a number of axioms was for centuries considered the model of scientific exposition. Of all the books that we have mentioned it is the least dated. For lovers of mathematics, it remains a magnificent book, imperishable as the dialogues of Plato or the dramas of Sophocles. We can imagine how seriously the great men of the seventeenth century whose goal it was to establish a new rational world picture based on the new commercial society and its science, studied these *Elements*, men like Stevin, Descartes, Spinoza and Huygens in the Netherlands. No teacher in our present schools will get the idea to teach from Aristotle, Ptolemy or Galen, but in geometry, knowingly or not, he will in his instruction be under the influence of Euclid, directly or indirectly.

With Archimedes, with whom in many respects the high point of scientific reasoning in antiquity was reached, the Latin Middle Ages were only poorly acquainted. It is rather interesting to note at this point that one of the first translators of some books of Archimedes into Latin (directly from the Greek) was Willem van Moerbeke, a Dominican born around 1220 in the Southern Netherlands. He lived for many years in Italy as a confidant of the Popes and translated also other Greek works into Latin, among them some of Aristotle. But only in the beginning of the new era interest in Archimedes begins to grow, in the first place in connection with the study of statics. Here again a man from the Netherlands belonged to the first to study Archimedes, and that was Stevin.

CHAPTER III

THE PERIOD OF TRANSITION

1

Towards the end of the fifteenth century the Latin-speaking world of scholars was pretty well acquainted with much of the best of the Greek and Arabic heritage, but was as yet unable to go beyond its level. If somebody like Avicenna or Omar Khayyam,[1] scientists from the eleventh and twelfth centuries, had reappeared in the Nuremberg or Venice of the time of Columbus, he would not have found much in the way of novelty except perhaps the admirable way of printing with movable type, the despicable way of spreading destruction and death with gun powder, or some other technical inventions, but new to them would have been the spirit of restless progress, not only among merchants, but also among craftsmen and men of learning, an atmosphere of fresh ideas on discovery and invention, on achieving more than their fathers, in sharp contrast to the more tradition-bound intellectual climate of the Orient.

By and by the critique of the old wisdom became more courageous, first usually where there was little chance of getting into conflict with the teachings of the Church, later also, if necessary, against the authorities. There was a current of thought preferring Plato to Aristotle, especially because Plato had shown greater preference for a mathematical approach. One of the first classical authors whose authority was attacked was Ptolemy: explorers from the Baltic region began to revise his geography of the North, Portuguese discoverers that of the South. With the discovery of Columbus of an "other world" in 1492, after 1507 more and more known as America, and the discovery of the sea route to India in

1498, the whole Ptolemaic geography was called into question. From the beginning of the sixteenth century on, maps appeared regularly with attempts to use this new knowledge, first in the form of amendments to Ptolemy, then more and more independent of him. Here Netherlanders played a leading role; the well-known world map of Mercator (1569) can be considered a kind of declaration of independence from Ptolemy.

The voyages of discovery did not only mean a revolution in geography. To Europe came new and surprising stories about unknown peoples, plants and animals. New demands were made on navigation and hence also on astronomy, on the theory of the magnet and on instrumentation. The physician obtained new medicines, farmer and gardener new plants. Manufacture and mining felt the influence, and even the theologians got new nuts to crack. All this accelerated the revolution that had already been in process for a long time. Growing towns had to solve new problems in architecture and public health. The building of canals, the art of warfare, of commerce and banking all had their own technical problems that often assumed a scientific character. The needs thus created often could not be satisfied by the old science, and the Aristotelian theories were often more a hindrance than a help. And then, after 1517, came the religious reformation that encouraged many, even those who, like Erasmus, wanted to stay inside the Catholic Church, to look at the traditional world outlook with a more critical eye, even where this outlook had intimate connections with theology.

It came to be in algebra that one of the first steps was taken to surpass in pure mathematics the limits of traditional science. In the early years of the sixteenth century the general solution of the third degree equations was found, a solution without the help of geometry, something which in those days was considered as a mighty step forward. At the present time this solution, discovered by scientists of Bologna, is a rather innocent and even boring part of our modern algebra, so that it is a little difficult to imagine how deeply this discovery stirred the minds. In Italy the public crowded to the disputations where leading mathematicians discussed the solution, often spiced by a mighty quarrel. When Cardano in 1545 published the new method, even together with the solution of the equations of the fourth degree, he called his book self-consciously the *Ars Magna*, the Great Art. Here were also the negative numbers, and later in the same century a professor in Bologna by the name of Bombelli even taught how to count with imaginaries. All these discoveries enriched the whole of arithmetic; an extensive literature with new symbolic methods spread over Europe. In Germany this new algebra was often called the rule of Coss (after the Italian word *cosa* for the unknown quantity, later written with the symbol x after Descartes). Lovers of arithmetic, also in the Netherlands, began to enjoy computations with numbers as well as algebraic symbols. The Hindu-Arabic decimal position system, now in general use, showed its great advantages over the abacus and the Roman numbers, though "reckoning on the lines" remained in use.

The *Ars Magna*, as already mentioned, dates from 1545. Two years earlier two books were published which even more than the *Ars Magna* introduced the new age in science. The first was written by a man from the Southern Netherlands named Andries van Wezel, better known as Andreas Vesalius; it opened a new period in medicine. The other was written by a man from Eastern Europe by the name of Copernicus and opened the period of the new astronomy. The revolution against medieval science was indeed on its way. Still another revolutionary book had appeared already in 1536: the *Institutio religionis Christianae* written by the Frenchman Calvin, a book making the Reformation much more attractive to the new mercantile classes than the semi-feudal Luther had ever been able to achieve. A remarkable dialectical turn in history has made the appearance of the intolerant Calvin, who in 1553 brought the learned Serveto, the doctor who announced the circulation of the blood, to the stake, a landmark in the history of the freedom of opinion.[2] In the long run those countries where Calvinism had made its deepest impression would play leading roles in the development of the new science. The Dutch Republic with its religious and intellectual tolerance is a good example.

Vesalius' book was called *De humani corporis fabrica* — 'On the Action of the Human Body'. He had studied at the University of Louvain and was for a while connected with the medical faculty of the University of Padua where, as we have seen before, a critical attitude with respect to Aristotle had existed for a long time. It was also here that fifty years later Galileo began to develop his ideas. Vesalius later became the personal physician of Charles V and his son Philip II; he died in 1564 at the age of fifty. The fame of his principal work lies especially in its refusal to repeat traditional book learning and its stress on independent experimentation, as we see already on the title page with a picture of an anatomical lesson with many onlookers. The book is famous for its beautiful illustrations rarely surpassed in medical books; these woodcuts are often attributed to the Renaissance painter Jan Steven van Kalkar, a pupil of Titian. The treatment of the muscles is especially successful; they are represented as they are situated under the skin in normal contraction. Vesalius always sees the body as a whole. There is something very modern in this book, we even find here a comparative investigation of different skulls. Yet, in many respects Vesalius still follows Galen, especially in his physiology. He could not follow his colleague Serveto in his proclamation of the circulation of the blood, though he already had reasonable objections to the opinion of Galen; he could not find the supposed aperture between the ventricles of the heart. After Vesalius, medical experimentation comes more and more to the fore and the authority of Galen is gradually waning.

Another anti-Galenic influence was the preaching and practice of the rather fantastic Swiss-German physician Theophrastus Paracelsus, a roving alchemist, astrologer and occultist, yet at the same time a pioneer breaking through ancient ways of thinking into real advances in chemistry and medicine. He rejected the theory of humors and introduced as natural elements the "chemical trias" of mercury, sulphur and salt, thus looking for the cause of diseases not in the upset of the balance of humors, but for specific causes in the mineral world, where he recommended as medicine materials such as mercury, sulphur, opium, iron and arsenic. For this reason there are people who consider him the "father" of pharmaceutical chemistry. In the years after his death in 1541 the Paracelsian mixture of what we now see as "proto-science" and science exercised a powerful influence on medicine and chemistry, setting in motion the search for new methods of therapy and medicines, with Cartesian rationalism gradually stripping this search from its occult elements, but never quite destroying them.

To the revolution in geography, mathematics and medicine we must add the revolution in astronomy, represented by Copernicus. In his system, announced in his *De Revolutionibus orbium celestium* — 'On the Revolution of the Celestial Bodies' — the earth experiences a double motion: a rotation around its axis and another one around a center not far from the sun. Around this center also rotate the other planets, but the moon turns around the earth. It is true that Copernicus, to save the phenomena, retains much of the epicycle theory of Ptolemy and that there are many medieval notions in his way of reasoning; his plea for a circular motion of the earth was based on Plato's theory that the circle is the perfect curve. After all, there was still no new dynamics. But his heliocentric system meant such a progress as compared to the geocentric system that Copernicus initiated a true revolution in thought by proclaiming the heliocentric system, not only as a possibility, but even as a fact. Some authors like to talk of Copernicus' "conservatism", because he retained so much from Ptolemy, just as we could speak of Vesalius' conservatism because he accepted so much from Galen or even of Columbus' conservatism because he continued to believe that he had reached Asia. The essential element in the discoveries made by these great men is, however, *the break at the right place* with the traditional opinions impeding the free study and understanding of the world, in such a way that others could continue to build on it.

Copernicus' work for many years did not make much of an impression because he could not do anything better for his system than appeal to its simplicity and Platonic beauty. The computation of astronomic tables did not depend on the truth of the Copernican system as it existed at that time. The immediate need for navigation and cartography was better observation, and in the second half of the sixteenth century this work was undertaken with great perseverance by the Dane Tycho Brahe. Such improved observations could also lead to improvement in the understanding of the world system, a feat actually accomplished by Tycho Brahe's pupil Kepler who in 1609 openly proclaimed the Copernican system in the sense that the planets move in ellipses around the sun, with the sun not in the center, but in the focus. Brahe himself had not too much confidence in the Copernican system and in 1583 presented as his own opinion that the earth stands in the center of the sphere of the fixed stars, that the sun turns around the earth, but that the planets turn about the sun, something more in accordance with Aristotelian physics (and theology). Yet also this statement was a break with traditional science. For years the three systems of Ptolemy, Brahe and Copernicus were taught side by side.

The Aristotelian theories continued to be doubted or attacked in almost all possible domains. The new practical mechanics to build canals, ships, pumps and cranes and to direct firearms could find little help from the old theories. Here Archimedes turned out to be of use, his mathematical methods at least as much as his results, since his only occupation had been with the equilibrium of bodies and liquids and not with the theory of motion. There was also a trend, at the University of Padua and elsewhere, to develop theories that would lead to our concept of inertia and therefore to a more quantitative approach. The result of this skepticism, or worse, with respect to Aristotle was a kind of scientific and philosophical anarchy, because for the time being only isolated criticism could be directed at the great and closed system of the great Greek philosopher — an anarchy in remarkable accordance with the political anarchy of those days of religious wars and assassinations. But criticism itself advanced rapidly; where Averroës had said in the twelfth century that nobody in fifteen hundred years had been able to add anything essential to the writings of Aristotle or discover in it one error of importance, Petrus Ramus, a young French mathematician, educator and philosopher, dared proclaim in 1536 openly that "everything taught by Aristotle is made out of whole cloth" — *Quaecumque ab Aristotele dicta essent, commentitia.* This judgment, later modified somewhat by Ramus when he became better acquainted with Aristotle, is of some interest to us because Ramus, who in 1572 was assassinated during the night of Saint Bartholomew, gained a great reputation in Holland till deep into the seventeenth century as a martyr of Protestantism, a reputation perhaps greater than he deserved if we take only his writings on mathematics and logic into account.

This was the intellectual revolution that accompanied the early development of capitalism. What would happen if this system were to solidify its stronghold and even to undermine the whole of feudalism? We get a clear picture of this if we look at the history of the sciences in the Dutch Golden Century.

2

The history of the sciences in the Netherlands concerns itself almost exclusively with the South, i.e., present Belgium, until the time of the new Republic. We have already mentioned Willem van Moerbeke, the thirteenth century native of Brabant, who translated Archimedes; one of the manuscripts that he translated was that on the equilibrium of submerged bodies that contains the well-known hydrostatic "law of Archimedes". Magister Jan Yperman of Bruges was a famous surgeon in the early part of the fourteenth century. Pierre d'Ailly, whose book of 1410 on the world picture (*Imago mundi*) was a special favorite of Columbus, was archbishop of Cambray. In 1425 Louvain became the seat of a university, then, as now, a bastion of Catholic theology, but also strong in medicine, for a long time in most universities the only faculty with room for the natural sciences. The Flemish painters of the Burgundian period such as the brothers van Eyck shared in the admiration for the new science of perspective invented by their Italian colleagues, though it seems that they did not advance in this type of geometry as far as the Italians. The mighty mercantile cities of Flanders, Ghent, Bruges, Ypres, Cambray had their physicians, accountants, teachers of mathematics and shared with the magnificent Burgundian court at Brussels its love for the arts. Musicians from the Netherlands were famous all over Europe, but it was only during the reign of Charles V, when Antwerp had become the richest city of the Netherlands, that in the present Belgium we meet men of science whose names are still well remembered. We have already mentioned Vesalius and Mercator, but they were not the only ones.

In cartography the great time in Belgium begins with Jemme Reiniersz, or Gemma Reyneri, a Frisian from Dokkum and therefore also called Frisius. From 1541 on he taught medicine at Louvain and died at the age of forty-seven — in those days men who lived longer than sixty years were a rarity. Gemma wrote a Latin *Arithmetica* that passed through a great number of reprints and from which whole generations of Latin scholars learned their elementary mathematics (first published in 1540), but his real merits lie in his work on scientific geography. A burning subject was the correct determination of latitude and longitude. Already Ptolemy had indicated means to achieve such a correct determination, but it required good instruments to measure time and angles, also some knowledge of astronomy and trigonometry and above all the scientific collaboration of observers at different points of the earth, and all this left much to be desired. Latitude can be determined by taking polar altitude and in the Northern hemisphere the polar star is quite close to the North Pole, but it was more convenient to measure the meridian altitude of the sun by which the polar altitude could be found by a simple computation, if the declination of the sun was known. For this purpose there existed already at an early date declination tables for every day, though they were far from accurate. In 1474 such tables had already been printed; they were due to the astronomer Regiomontanus from Nuremberg. Others followed.

The permanent problem was the determination of longitude or better the longitude difference between a point on earth and a fixed meridian. For this it was necessary to have either good clocks or observers who watched the same celestial phenomenon at different places and then compared their local times. Such a celestial phenomenon was, so to speak, a celestial clock. An example was a lunar eclipse. Gemma knew this and tried to do something about it. He proposed corrections in the existing instruments for angle measurements, of which the so-called astrolabe, the cross staff and the quadrant were the principal ones. He also proposed, in 1530, to use as clocks the portable timepieces working with a spring and fusee, invented not so long before and known as Nuremberg eggs. That made rather good sense on land, but it was impossible at sea; for this the eggs were still too primitive. Gemma also proposed to establish over a particular territory a net of precisely measured triangles, the so-called triangulation, indeed at that time and long after the only method to get precise regional maps (1533). His methods may well have been applied by Jacob van Deventer in his for his time remarkably correct Dutch provincial maps (1536–1546), and by other cartographers who followed his example. The first triangulation of which we are certain and know details is that of Snellius in the next century, with much better instruments than van Deventer possessed.

Gemma himself also constructed maps and even globes, but his principal merit in this field has been the inspiration he gave to a brilliant pupil, Gerardus Mercator. Mercator, which is Latin for *Kremer* (merchant), was born in 1512 in Rupelmonde (Flanders) and learned his trade in Louvain under Frisius. In 1552 he left for Duisburg on the Rhine after having been accused of heresy. There he remained as the head of the most famous cartographic house of his time until his death in 1594. In 1538 his first world map appeared in a curious "cordiform" projection, where the surface of the earth is laid out in the form of a heart. This map still shows clearly the unsatisfactory knowledge of non-European countries typical for the first half-century after Columbus, not particularly furthered by the secretive attitudes of the different governments. But Mercator's fame is due primarily to his beautiful large world map, his *mappamundi* of 1569, the result of years of work in obtaining information from all kinds of sources, in a projection used to the present day, especially for maps of large sections of the earth, the so-called Mercator projection. For the first time we meet a world map in which, despite all defects, we recognize the surface of our earth. The net of meridians and parallels is rectangular and rectilinear, and the parallels move away from each other towards the north and the south of the equator so that lines of equal course, the rhumb lines, are represented by straight lines. This principle also prevailed on the ancient *portolani* maps, but this time certain mathematical rules were followed according to what we now call conformal representation — on a Mercator map angles between directions on earth remain the same, so that small areas are faithfully represented, but distortion of large territories is increased the more we approach the arctic and antarctic regions. The result is that Canada, Greenland and Siberia look much larger than they are in reality. The mathematical theory of the Mercator map was not simple, so that, for instance, captains who wanted to sail along a great circle on the sphere (the shortest way between two points) could not find their way on such a map, since a great circle (except a meridian) does not project as a straight line. For many years the Mercator map was mostly a toy for learned men till experience, better mathematics and better knowledge of its use made it one of the most popular of all maps of the oceans of the world as a whole.

Mercator was also one of the first to publish a complete book of maps. He called his book *Atlas* after a mythical figure sometimes described as a giant carrying the earth on his shoulders, sometimes as a noble king, protector of the sciences. The *Atlas* was often reprinted in Amsterdam where Mercator's son-in-law Jodocus Hondius had established himself in 1595, after a stay in London where his work included the etching of maps for the English edition of Waghenaer's "Mirror" (see p. 37).

Antwerp in the days of Charles V and afterwards till the end of the century, was the richest mercantile town of the Netherlands and a center of international commerce. Here the mercantile sciences were in vogue, the arts of navigation, mathematics, cosmography and book-keeping. Here Abraham Ortelius, Mercator's friend, had his cartographic house where already in 1571 he produced an "Atlas" with the title *Theatrum orbis terrarum* with strong Mercator influence. There were also many printing establishments, among them the famous house of Plantin, started in 1555, still remembered in Antwerp in the museum Plantin-Moretus. Many scientific books, large and small, were printed and published here, mostly in Latin, French or Flemish, sometimes inspired

Willem Blaeu's globe (*Ver. Nederlandsch Historisch Scheepvaart Museum, Amsterdam*).

A Flemish astrolabe made by Michael Coignet (1549–1623) in Antwerp
(*Museum Boerhaave, Leiden*).

A Vesalius. Title page of his pioneer work *De humani corporis fabrica* (1543)
(*Museum Boerhaave, Leiden*).

Petrus Plancius at age seventy, in 1622. Engraving by W. Delff (1623)
(*Museum Boerhaave, Leiden*).

De Groote LICHTENDE ofte Vyerighe Colom

Over de Zee Custen
Van 't Wester/ Ooster/ en Noorder Vaer-water.
Met Privilegie, voor Achthien Jaeren.

t'AMSTELREDAM
By Iacob Aertsz. Colom, Boeckverkooper op 't Water/
In de Vyerighe Colom/ Anno 1652.

Lecture on navigation by the Reverend P. Plancius in the Old Side Chapel, Amsterdam
(*Ver. Nederlandsch Historisch Scheepvaart Museum, Amsterdam*).

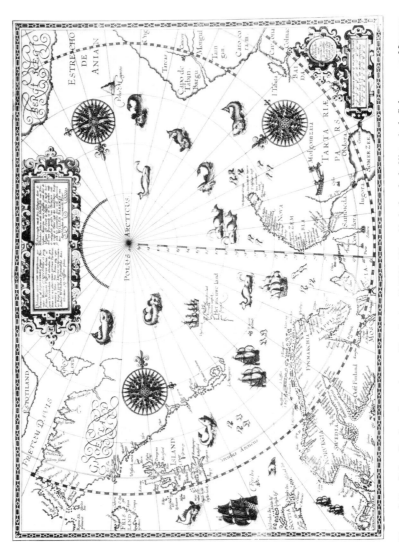

Map of the Polar Region, from J. van Linschoten (1599) (*Ver. Nederlandsch Historisch Scheepvaart Museum, Amsterdam*).

WILLEBRORDUS SNELLIUS,
Matheseos Professor.

Willebrord Snellius (1586–1626) (*Museum Boerhaave, Leiden*).

Jan Adriaansz. Leeghwater (1575–1650) (*Museum Boerhaave, Leiden*).

by Spanish or German models. One of the authors was Michel Coignet, teacher of arithmetic and navigation, who wrote in French and whose books were widely read. One copy was found in 1871 in the ruins of the house on Novaya Zemlya where Willem Barendsz. and his mates had left it after being compelled to spend the winter of 1596/97 on that barren island.[3]

This flowering of the Southern Netherlands came to an end with the disturbances under the Spanish occupation, and in particular after the coming of Alva in 1567 and his reign of terror, again followed by other violence (the so-called Spanish and French Furies of 1576 and 1583). Especially after the fall of Antwerp to the Spanish in 1585 thousands of South Netherlanders, many of them Calvinists, left their homeland to find in other countries an existence with less violence and more freedom of conscience. Mercator had been one of the first to go; he went to Germany together with many others, among them the merchant family of Bernoulli which would produce in the next centuries a whole family of mathematicians and other scientists. Others fled to England, among them the merchant-historian Emanuel van Meteren and the physician-botanist Mathias De L'Obell after whom that pretty flower, the Lobelia, is named. But many moved north to the new Republic, where we shall meet many who became prominent in trade, theology, humanism and the sciences: Stevin, Plancius, Lansbergen, Moucheron, Marolois, van Schooten. Few despotic gentlemen have damaged their own cause as much as Don Fernando Alvarez de Toledo, 3rd Duke of Alva.

We should not think, however, that this exodus, certainly damaging to the country, was a mortal blow to Belgian science. But it did change its character. Under the Spanish archdukes it assumed in part a courtly-clerical appearance, instead of being, as before, a science serving navigation, surveying and commerce. After the conquest of Antwerp by the Spanish the Jesuits entered the city, spiritual soldiers of the counter-Reformation, skilled in diplomacy, education and science. Among them we find during the seventeenth century some excellent mathematicians as François d'Aguillon, architect and author of a book on perspective well known at that time (1613); followed later in the century by Grégoire de Saint Vincent and André Tacquet, both important in the prehistory of the integral calculus. There were also important scientists not affiliated with the order. Among them we find Adriaan van Roomen (Romanus), first professor of mathematics at Louvain, then, from 1593 to 1607, teacher of mathematics and medicine in Würzburg, where Willebrord Snellius was his pupil. Van Roomen was one of those mathematicians in the course of the centuries occupied with the so-called problem of Apollonius to construct a circle tangent to three given circles. He computed π to 16 decimals.[4] Another, even more outstanding, figure is Johannes Baptista van Helmont, physician and chemist, like Paracelsus a century before. Of patrician stock, he received his medical degree at Louvain and after some years of travel settled first for seven years at Vilvoorde north of Brussels, then from 1616 to his death in 1644 in Brussels itself. His ideas, strongly influenced by Paracelsus, have that same flavor of "proto-science" and modern experimental research that is typical of his predecessor, and again the modern side has been the more lasting. During his lifetime he was for years the target of Catholic theologians objecting to what they suspected as the work of the devil in some of his occultist ideas, but they do not seem to have interfered with his experimentation. He was especially interested in the study of fermentation, advocated chemical medicines and discredited the Galenic theory of humors in favor of an understanding of the nature of individual diseases as determined by specific agents. With Paracelsus he is therefore often viewed as one of the precursors of the iatrochemists (see Chapter IX) as well as a precursor of pharmaceutical chemistry. To him we owe the word 'gas' as the "spirit that cannot be preserved in vessels nor be reduced to a visible body", a name first given to carbon dioxide.

In the Belgium of those days we also meet the astronomer Michel-Florent van Langren, from a family of cartographers with members also in Amsterdam, one of the first to construct a lunar map (1645). This was not just for fun; he wanted to facilitate the determination of geographical longitude, an idea, as we have seen, typical for this century. The lunar disc as a whole was too inaccurate a "celestial clock", so that it was much better to tabulate an exact point, say a mountain on the moon. We do not hear of any practical application of this idea, not even on land. But in the history of lunar maps, which begins with the sketches of Galileo in his *Sidereus Nuncius* of 1610, this lunar map of the Belgian scientist is of some importance, since, together with the map of the Danzig astronomer Hevelius of 1647, reproduced by the Italian Riccioli in 1651, it belongs to the first maps to introduce a geographical nomenclature on the moon.

We shall talk later in this book about Wenzel Cobergher and his engineering work. But we still must return for a moment to our Belgian Jesuits, and mention how some of them, emulating the Italian Father Matteo Ricci, contributed to the introduction of Western scientific ideas into China (but not the Copernican system) and in turn brought information on Chinese customs and science to Western Europe, thus enlarging in their own way the cultural outlook of both parts of the world.

We see therefore that the Spanish domination of the Southern Netherlands did not prevent some good science to maintain itself. However, to obtain a thorough understanding of the great adventures of seventeenth-century science we have to look at the North, where after the declaration of independence in 1581 that wonderfully new and lively period begins that we call the Golden Century.

CHAPTER IV

THE DUTCH TEACHERS OF MATHEMATICS AND NAVIGATION

1

We should not think that during the centuries preceding the rise of the Dutch Republic, the Northern Netherlands were inhabited only by semi-illiterates in the service of feudal princes always at each others' throats. We only have to look at the noble lines of the Knights Hall (*Ridderzaal*) in The Hague or the townhalls of Middelburg and Gouda to understand how much taste existed in the Holland and Zeeland of these days, not to speak of the beauty of some of the churches. Dutch prosperity depended to a considerable degree on the herring fishery that flourished because an invention called *haringkaken*, a special conservation method of gutting, salting and barreling ascribed to Willem Beukelsz. of Biervliet in Zeeland around 1300. The coastal trade was a good school for the training of skippers and shipbuilders, the preserving of dykes and drainage for that of mill builders and engineers. Connections with the Hansa broadened vision and the sense of toleration. We may be sceptical of the story that not Gutenberg in Mainz, but Laurens Jansz. Coster in Haarlem invented printing with movable type, but it illustrates the fact that this process was developed in the Netherlands at an early date (after ca. 1450). Literacy was widespread. There were many schools that were as good as we may expect for their period, among which those conducted by the Brethren of the Common Life, organized in the fourteenth century, enjoyed a certain amount of fame and are still remembered. It is true that when these Brethren meditated with a book in a quiet corner, this book might well have been an edifying one with a touch of Ruusbroec mysticism, such as the *Imitation of Christ* ascribed to Brother Thomas à Kempis of Wildesheim near Zwolle. But some schools, among them especially the one at Deventer, had scientific or at any rate humanistic pretensions; one of the pupils at Deventer was the cardinal Nicholas Cusanus, who became one of the best fifteenth century mathematicians, cosmographers and philosophers. Erasmus was one of the scholars attending this school under the rectorate of the Westphalian Alexander Hegius (1463– 1490), a scholar and poet active in reforming Latin education, giving it a more humanistic direction and adding Greek to the curriculum. Sometimes, it is said, he had more than two thousand pupils. Deventer, a Hansa city on the Ysel, an arm of the Rhine, thus deserves our attention as a modest cultural center away from the leading towns near the North Sea, probably more important than rival Kerkrade in Limburg with its abbey Kloosterrade or Rolduc and the claim, incidentally, of being the oldest mining town in Europe, with coal digging already reported in the twelfth century. Both centers were under the aegis of a bishop see, Deventer under Utrecht, Kerkrade under Liège. Utrecht itself has scientific traditions going back to bishop Adalbold of the early part of the eleventh century, a cleric in correspondence with the mathematically inclined Gerbert of Aurillac, later Pope Sylvester II. To the circle of Gerbert pupils belonged also Franco of Liège, interested in the quadrature of the circle (ca. 1150). All this mathematical interest was rather amateurish, the Greek heritage was still largely unknown, the authority mainly Boethius. This Adalbold was also the rebuilder of the church of Saint Martin, the precursor of the present Dom church in Utrecht; we can imagine him supervising the work with a Gerbert abacus in his hand.

When, in the second half of the fifteenth century, the bishop chair in Utrecht was occupied by a prince of the Burgundian house, his castle at Wijk-bij-Duurstede on an arm of the Rhine (a ruin remains today) was, culturally, a reflection of the splendid court

at Brussels. Deventer, in his day, as we noticed, was already one
of the towns engaged in the printing trade. The first arithmetic
for use in schools in the Northern Netherlands was published there
in 1557, written in the vernacular by teacher Maarten Creszfeld.[2]
The oldest mathematician in the North of some distinction, Claes
Pietersz, likewise hailed from Deventer. We already mentioned
the cartographer Jacob van Deventer whose name also suggests
a connection with the city on the Ysel. During the days of Charles
V and Philip II he designed more than 250 city and provincial
maps; many of them have been preserved and are not only a pleasure to the eye, but are treasure trove for antiquarian topographers.

The bitter truth, however, is that distinguished Dutchmen from
the North with scientific ambitions preferred as a rule to run
away from the country, following the example of Erasmus. The
Southern Netherlands under the Burgundians and the Habsburgs
had more attractions. We know the trend from the artists; Jan
van Eyck went from the Hague to the South, and so did Dirc
Bouts from Haarlem, both during Burgundian days. During the
reign of Charles V we find Jacob van Deventer after 1536 in
Brabant, where he probably found inspiration from Gemma
Frisius; we have already followed Frisius himself from Friesland
to Louvain. Hans Vredeman de Vries, born 1514 in Leeuwarden
in Friesland, architect, painter and mathematician, wandered all
over Central Europe, employed part of the time by the emperor
Rudolph at Prague, till he returned in his old days and found re-
cognition in his home country. Volcher Koyter (or Coiter, Coyter),
born 1534 at Groningen, was a pupil of Vesalius' successor at
Padua, Gabriele Falloppio (after whom the uterine tubes are
named), and worked as a physician in Italy, France and Germany.
He composed the first topological and anatomical atlas of the
human body (1572) and studied the poison gland of the adder,
skeletons of birds and the development of the human and animal
embryo, especially that of the chicken in the egg, so that he can be

seen as a pioneer in comparative anatomy as well as embryology. Some of his works have been republished in 1955.

Among the reformers of the calendar in this period we also find a runaway Dutchman, a man from Zeeland called Paulus van Middelburg. After studying in Louvain, he became bishop of Fossombrone in Italy. As an astronomer he participated in the Lateran Council of 1512–1517 that took steps to replace the antiquated Julian calendar by a better one, a plan only realized under Gregory XIII in 1582, when the date sprang overnight from October 4 to October 15 (in his bull *Inter gravissimas*).[3] After he had left Zeeland, Paulus muttered that in that country only drunkenness is praised as highest virtue, *in qua ebrietas sola ut virtus summa laudatur*. This was not quite fair, but we must not forget that the North at that time was far from being an attractive place for a meditating mind. The final struggles between the old feudal order and the centralizing power from Brussels brought incessant plunder and murder in raids and counter-raids, connected with the, in the Netherlands, still well-remembered names of Grote Pier and Maarten van Rossum, *condottieri* in service of the duke of Gelderland. Those who preferred to stick it out might share the fate of the good humanist-poet-educator Johannes Murmellius, pupil of Hegius in Deventer, later rector of the Latin school at Alkmaar, who saw his school and house go up in flames during one of these raids and, barely saving his life, lost it only a few weeks later in Zwolle. The name of doctor Johannes Wier (or Weyer) also reminds us of the savagery of these days. Returned from study abroad at the age of twenty-five, he practiced in Grave and Arnhem and was, after 1555, physician at the court of the humanist count William of Gulik and Cleve. His fame is based on his protest against the violent witch-craze of his day; especially through his book *De prestigiis daemonum* (1563, 1577), in which he asked for medical examination rather than torture in the case of persons accused of witchcraft.

Some progress is gradually made. The painter Cornelisz. Anthonisz.[4] in Amsterdam, a contemporary of Jacob van Deventer, did cartographical work of considerable merit. During the years marking the beginning of the struggle for independence the first school books on arithmetic appear in the Northern Netherlands, that of Creszfeld and Claes Pietersz. (1567), already mentioned, and of Hobbe Jacobsz. Helmduyn (1569), the latter two in Amsterdam. Claes Pietersz., or Nicholas Petri Daventriensis, as he called himself, for years dominated the market with his writings on mathematics and navigation. In 1583 his *Practique om te leren rekenen, cypheren ende boeckhouden met die regel Coss en Geometrie* (A Practical Method to learn how to Count, Cypher and Keep Books with the Rule of Coss and with Geometry) already in the title announces the large number of subjects in which this teacher, then in Amsterdam, gave instruction, and the content shows that he was very well versed in the mathematics of his day. We should also not forget Adriaen Anthonisz., the plucky burgomaster of Alkmaar, a military and hydraulic engineer, adviser to William and Maurice of Orange in the technique of fortification. He too has kept his little niche in mathematics, where the value of $\pi = \frac{355}{113}$ is connected with his name, usually as the value of Metius after the name accepted by his sons — by the way, a value that the Chinese had already known for many centuries.

2

This was a modest beginning. It is surprising to see how much the intellectual situation changes after 1581, when the Republic of the Seven Provinces comes into existence. It is a phenomenon that we repeatedly meet in history in the aftermath of a revolution — in the United States after 1783, in England after 1642, in France after 1789 and in Russia after 1917. The young Republic already possessed a university at Leiden, founded in 1575, which could soon pride itself on some of the most eminent scholars in Europe, often brought in from abroad as Scaliger and Clusius. There was scientific activity in many towns and from this activity sprang at least three books that became well known all over Europe: Stevin's books on the *Thiende* (1585) and the *Weeghconst* (1586) and Waghenaer's *Spieghel der Zeevaert* (1584–1585) – all three not in Latin but in the vernacular. We shall leave Stevin till the next chapter and deal here with Waghenaer.

The old coastal traffic had resumed its former vigor. The time had come to learn from the Spanish and the Flemish, already for a long period engaged in publishing charts and books helpful to the art of navigation. Help came from the widely travelled and experienced pilot Lucas Jansz. Waghenaer from Enkhuizen. His *Spieghel der Zeevaert*, published in Leiden by the famous house of Plantin, founded in Antwerp and recently also established in the North, did not only offer a readable text for pilots, but the best sea charts from the Baltic to Spain and can be considered the first sea atlas.[5] This book was followed in 1592 by the *Thresoor der Zeevaert* (Treasury of Navigation), collected with the *Spieghel* in 1598 in the *Enchuyser Zeevaertbook*. This was indeed a book that filled an existing gap; the *Spieghel* was translated into French, English and Latin and was not only reprinted many times, but also imitated. The story is told that Waghenaer's atlas, in the hands of the English admirals, contributed to the victory over the Spanish Armada in 1588. Translated into English as *Mirrour of Navigation*, the book stimulated the publication of all kinds of "mirrors". Even more, the name Waghenaer, anglicized into Waggoner, remained in England for a long time the general name for a guide to navigation. There are not so many proper names that have passed into the spoken language, such a maecenas and caesar (Kaiser, tsar) with a desire to honor, or as martinet and quisling, leaving a feeling of disgust. Lynch and boycott are other examples. Enkhuizen has had its celebrities indeed.

From Enkhuizen also came good advice for the Great Traffic, developed under the influence of the Middelburg shipowner Balthasar de Moucheron. Like so many young fellows from the Netherlands, Jan Huygen van Linschoten had been in Spanish and Portuguese service and had spent several years in Goa as clerk to the Portuguese archbishop. On his travels, which also brought him for two years to the Azores, he eagerly collected all kinds of facts and data. Back in Enkhuizen he wrote down his experiences, and in 1596 published with Cornelis Claesz. in Amsterdam his *Itinerario, Voyage ofte schipvaert naar Oost oft Portugaals Indien 1579–1592* (Itinerary, voyage or navigation to East or Portuguese India). The publisher Claesz., like Moucheron an immigrant from the South, must, with Plantin, be remembered as a solid support for the budding science of the young Republic. The *Itinerario* was preceded by Linschoten's *Reys-Geschrift* (Travel story) of 1595. Both books, with their charts and pictures, written in pithy vernacular, were studied assiduously by all who were interested in the Great Traffic, and not only in the Netherlands, as we can see when we consult the famous English "Voyages" by Richard Hakluyt, published 1589 and later. Though he never travelled to America, Linschoten also tried to give his compatriots information concerning the new continent and for this purpose translated a big Spanish book about the "Indies" into Dutch.[6] There exists a notable parallel between the role played by Linschoten of Holland and that played by his contemporary Hakluyt in England as persons, or if you like to say prophets, in whetting the appetite for adventures overseas. We can understand how the "Hakluyt Society" in England, founded in order to publish ancient travel journals, has been followed by the "Linschoten Society" in the Netherlands. Lovers of ancient voyages of discovery and pithy sixteenth- and seventeenth-century vernacular can find plenty of armchair entertainment in the piles of books published by these societies.

The first Dutch voyage to the East Indies took place between 1595 and 1597 under the leadership of the two brothers Cornelis and Frederik de Houtman from Gouda, who had learned the trade from the Portuguese. Financial support came from Amsterdam merchants organized in the "Compagnie van Verre" (Company for faraway lands). Scientific support came primarily from *dominee* (minister) Platevoet, better known as Petrus Plancius. Plancius, a strong Calvinist, had immigrated from the South and had become a prominent minister of the Amsterdam Reformed Church. Here he preached the orthodox gospel, struggling valiantly against Catholic, Jewish, Socinian, Pelagian, and above all Arminian heresies. He must have been a man of enormous energy, studying all geographical documents he could lay his hands on, whether in print or manuscript, taught the art of navigation, prepared charts and globes, examined pilots and was the scientific advisor of all merchants and companies that participated in the Great Traffic. No wonder that evil tongues told of this man who

... through pulpit and advice did far more harm and pain, than hordes of regiments to wicked Pope and Spain ... [7]

that from the pulpit he told his audience sometimes more about America and the Indies than about Divine Grace. We do not know where he got his knowledge of cartography, but he must have informed himself remarkably well during his open-air preaching in the South.[8] His first world map appeared in 1590 and was followed by many others. Well known in his day was his large world map of 1592, following in general the map of Mercator, but without increasing degrees of latitude, so that, for instance, a section of the earth's surface of 10 degrees in latitude and 10 degrees in longitude was rendered everywhere by the same rectangle. Plancius' maps of different parts of the world like the Indian Archipelago and West Africa belong to the best drawn up to that time. He also constructed celestial globes and helped other people in making them. And so we see on the globe made by Mercator's son-in-law, Jodocus Hondius, of 1600, a number of new Southern constellations probably obtained from Plancius. This is likely because Plancius received the log books of the company pilots and studied them, and in this way he got under his eyes the observations of the Southern constellations performed by Pieter Dirckz. Keyser, chief pilot of the Houtman expedition. Keyser, a pupil of Plancius, and one of the earliest European observers of the Southern celestial hemisphere, died in 1596 during the expedition. He studied the sky from high up in the crow's nest.

Plancius also made himself known because of his prescriptions to determine differences in longitude at sea with the aid of the magnetic needle. We have already seen how many difficulties there were in the determination of longitude. It had been known for a long time that only at a few places on earth the magnetic needle points directly to the North. Columbus had discovered that such a place existed in the ocean not far from the Azores, and from this time on a whole literature had been produced about the possibility of determining the difference in longitude of a place and the line of deviation 0, the so-called agonic line. For simplicity's sake, the agonic line was taken to be a meridian and the deviation of the magnetic needle, the so-called declination, more or less proportional to the difference in longitude. This was a charming theory; a way to determine the difference in longitude from purely physical relations on earth independent of clocks and eclipses! But it did not work out very well, and Mercator had already found out that the magnetic North Pole does not coincide with the North Pole of the earth, as can be seen on his map of 1569.

Plancius, who urged all his pupils to perform magnetic observations, had a theory that postulated four agonic meridians with gradual increase and decrease of declination between them. He had constructed an instrument for it, modelled on Gemma Frisius' "astrolabium catholicum" with a table on which pilots could find the longitude as derived from latitude and declination. Plancius' methods and those of others were widely debated; one of the results was Stevin's *Havenvindingh* (How to Find the Harbor), taking from Plancius his more sober ideas: in the neighborhood of the coasts knowledge of latitude and declination could help in finding the right harbor. Since the declination is far more variable than Plancius realized, especially in the Arctic, he had in the long run very little success with the sailors; a report of 1611 concluded that Plancius' rule was "imperfect and entirely frivolous".

This has also been the judgment of history, but the discussions did have their use. They were one of the reasons that William Gilbert, physician to Queen Elizabeth, began to look at the whole question of magnetism with the eye of a modern man of science. This led to his book *De magnete* of 1600, one of the pioneer works in the new science of nature. Gilbert experimented with the "terella", a miniature magnetized terrestrial sphere, and reached the conclusion that the determination of longitude with the aid of deviation of the magnetic needle could hardly be successful. Gilbert also studied the inclination, i.e., the deviation of the magnet in the vertical plane and fostered some hope that this inclination could perhaps be of some help in the determination of latitude. As the seventeenth century advances, we hear less and less of determination with the aid of the needle and the attention shifts again to the ancient method: to find improved terrestrial or celestial clocks. Much of the research of Huygens in Holland (and France) was related to the solution of this problem.

3

Plancius' recommendations concerning the traffic to India led to lasting results. In the confusing geography of those days with their contradictions on the form of the continents he had his own way to reach conclusions. We thus find his name connected with the different "Passages" undertaken to reach the Orient from the Low Countries by sea.

Four possibilities existed: two around Asia, two around America; the two to the South unsafe because of the Spanish and Portuguese; the two to the North because of snow and ice. All four "Passages" were investigated by sailors from Holland and Zeeland during the early years of the Republic. True, only one of the four led in the long run to great financial profits, but all brought important scientific results. The South-East passage around the Cape of Good Hope, discovered in 1498 by Vasco Da Gama, was first undertaken by the Houtmans in 1595–1597 and led to the foundation of the East Indian colonial empire. The South-West Passage around South America, found in 1521–1522 by Magellan, was first undertaken by Olivier van Noort in 1598. It led in 1616 to the discovery of Cape Horn (Hoorn) by Willem Cornelisz. Schouten and Jacques Le Maire and with this to the proof that Fireland (Tierra del Fuego) is separated by the ocean from the supposed "Southland" (Terra Australis), in contradiction to the teachings of Mercator. A map will tell us that to get to Cape Horn from the East you may have to pass through the Strait of Le Maire.

The possibility of the Northern Passages was based on the hypothesis that between America and East Asia there existed somewhere to the North a sea passage, called the Strait of Anian, named after a passage in Marco Polo. It was indicated on Mercator's map of 1569. The English had already tried more than once to reach that Strait of Anian, either to the East around Asia or to the West around America. Due to the severe climate of the Arctic seas these attempts had failed, but also brought a positive result, namely the opening of the trade between England and Russia via the White Sea. The Dutch wanted to profit likewise from this trade and, moreover, to continue the voyages as far as the Strait of Anian.

The best-known of these voyages undertaken under Plancius' scientific direction is the one under Jacob van Heemskerck and Willem Barendsz. in 1596—1597, that led to the bitter winter on Novaya Zemlya.[9] Later, in 1609, the English captain Henry Hudson, an Englishman in Dutch service, also tried the North-East Passage, but, halted by ice and mutiny, turned around and tried the North-West Passage. Sailing along the American coast he inspected the large river, called the North River by the Dutch, and now known as the Hudson river. At the mouth of this river, in 1626, the newly-founded West India Company founded the settlement of New Amsterdam, the beginning of the Dutch colonial empire in North America, lost to the English later in the century, when New Amsterdam became New York, where up to the present time its Dutch origin is kept in remembrance. We shall return to it in a later chapter.

Barendsz. owed his authority as a pilot not only to his voyages, but also to his knowledge of theoretical navigation and his *Caertboeck*, a book of maps of the Mediterranean (1595) with an instruction in navigation and cartography. A clever supplement to the *Spieghel* of Waghenaer, it represented a new kind of Dutch enterprise, the traffic into the Mediterranean, seriously undertaken only after 1590. The map is of interest because it contained sailing directions and is one of the first carrying magnetic data. Purchas, the successor of Hakluyt as the English compiler of travel stories, also paid attention to the travels of Barendsz.

In those days there was a lot of talk and speculation about the real or imagined existence of the Strait of Anian, the climate, the territorial division and the animals of the polar regions. This was in connection with the discovery of Spitsbergen by Barendsz. in 1596, the island character of Novaya Zemlya and the possibility of an open polar sea. (Mercator surrounded the North Pole by four large islands.) One of the practical results of these discussions was the flowering of the whaling enterprise in these northern waters.

The Strait of Anian turned out to be a reality in its own way, but only after its discovery by the Russians in the eighteenth century. We now know the Bering Strait as the reality behind the story of the Strait of Anian.

The first bold expeditions led to many others, leading to the discovery of many data on nature and peoples, as well as the improvement of the maps of the coasts of America and the islands of the East Indian archipelago. The best-remembered of these voyages of discovery are those of Abel Jansz. Tasman, sent by the Governor-General of the Indies, Anthonie van Diemen, in 1642–1644 to the more or less hypothetical "Southland" (Terra Australis). Tasman discovered by sailing around it that the Southland really existed and formed a continent by itself that we now know by the name of Australia. These travels have given their name to Van Diemen's Land and to Tasmania. Tasman is also the "discoverer" (the Maoris had already discovered that country several centuries before) of New Zealand, where we have a Tasman Sea and the Tasman mountains. The world map has many names that remind us of the discoveries of the Republic: Cape Horn (Hoorn) and Cape Hinlopen, Block Island and Brooklyn (Breukelen), Flushing (Vlissingen), Staten Island, Strait of Le Maire and Schoutensland, Mauritius, Spitsbergen, Jan Mayenland, New Zealand, the Barents Sea, Stellenbosch, and many others. It still seems to be a moot point whether Rhode Island got its name from the Dutch (Red Island), or from a romantic association with the isle of Rhodes.[10]

All these discoveries were used by the Dutch cartographers to make their maps the best in the world. The pioneering work of Waghenaer, Plancius and their colleagues was the beginning of the great period in Dutch cartography. After the death of Mercator in 1594 his son-in-law Jodocus Hondius transferred the house to Amsterdam where it continued under the son-in-law of Hondius, Jan Jansz. or Johannes Jansonius. One of the principal productions of this house was an improved *Atlas* of Mercator that now replaced the *Theatrum* of Ortelius on the market. There were also competitors. The most important among them was the house of Willem Jansz. Blaeu, whose *Tooneel des Aerdrycks* (The Terrestrial Stage) (1634–1635) with a text in Dutch, French, German and Latin was widely used. Blaeu was also famous for his beautiful terrestrial and celestial globes, some of which still can be admired in musea. His shops were found on the Bloemgracht and the Damrak in Amsterdam and were tourist attractions; his and the other cartographic enterprises in Amsterdam were models for the whole international industry. The maps of Blaeu, Hondius, Jansonius, Visscher and other Dutchmen with their pretty colors and baroque ornaments are still much appreciated by lovers both of history and of art and can be admired on the walls of many a museum or private home either as originals or in colored reproductions. Only after 1650 with Nicolas Sanson's example, followed by Guillaume Delisle, the French enter the stage as serious competitors, and deservedly so. The Dutch map makers indulged a little too much in reprinting their old maps without critical discernment, so that these maps became somewhat out of date in geography and nomenclature. On some Dutch maps published late in the seventeenth century Boston Harbor in Massachusetts was still indicated by the name Vishaven (fish harbor), a name invented in 1614 by Adriaen Block (comp. Chapter X) long before there was a Boston in existence. But it was not only the maps that made Dutch publishing firms so famous in their day. Blaeu was also a general bookseller and publisher and so were also Plantin, Elzevier, van Waesberge, Cornelis Claesz. and others whose author lists contained some of the best-known European scholars and scientists of their day. Many of these books published by these firms are still bearing witness to the tolerance and good taste of the Golden Century. The Dutch art of publishing and cartography is one of the bridges built to carry us from the land of Stevin and Huygens to that of Rembrandt.

4

The maps of the Netherlands could never have been so good without experienced surveyors and these could not have come into
being without good teachers of mathematics and instrument makers. The economic development of the Republic was closely
related to the skill of these men; there was no mercantile town in
which they did not have an important function. They were often
men from the people, sometimes former sailors, sometimes im-
migrants from Flanders or Germany, self-made without much
knowledge of Latin, as well as wine gaugers, surveyors, school-
teachers or engineers. There doubtlessly were quacks among them,
but also intelligent and well-read fellows, tireless calculators with
the beautiful and powerful decimal position system, resourceful
with hands and tools, engravers, writers of pamphlets and books,
and even in their own way men of literature and homespun
wisdom. They had their professional pride and could occasionally
quarrel noisily as befits competitors. In the long run every town
of some importance produced its own school books, big or small,
some showing considerable erudition such as those of Claesz.
Pietersz. They belonged to the middle class, the *burghers*, but
rarely to the patricians, among whom the class of regents already
began to form a rather close caste in itself. As famous as Claesz.
Pietersz. in his day, if not more famous, was Ludolf van Ceulen,
a fencing master from Delft and a native of Hildesheim in Germany. Between his fencing lessons to the sons of rich merchants
he taught arithmetic and geometry, carried out mercantile computation or, for his own pleasure, went in for research of greater
depth. In his book *Van den Circkel* (1596, reprinted 1615),
later translated into Latin by Snellius, he computed the number
π to twenty decimals, in his time a *tour de force* of patience,
because he had to compute the side of a regular polygon of
32,512,254,720 sides. Later he continued the computation and

reached thirty-five decimals. Because of this some people still call this number π the Ludolfian number, especially in Germany. In 1600, our fencing master was called to Leiden as a teacher at the engineering school founded under the auspices of Maurice of Orange, a school where instruction was given in the native language. Here he died in 1610. The 35 decimals could for many years be seen on his tombstone in the Pieter Church; a part of the stone still exists as part of a column.

Van Ceulen was a friend and protégé of the Delft burgomaster Jan Cornets de Groot, a man with a great interest in the exact sciences, whom we shall meet as a friend of Stevin. His merits have been somewhat obscured by the glory of his son, the great Latinist and lawyer Hugo de Groot or Grotius whose statue graces the market place of Delft in front of the Nieuwe Kerk with the ornamental tomb of the Orange princes.

A distinguished surveyor was Jan Pietersz. Dou in Leiden who made Euclid's geometry available in Dutch (1606). Equally distinguished was Ezechiel de Decker, whom we meet around 1626 in Gouda and later in Rotterdam. De Decker and Vlacq are often mentioned in connection with the early computation of logarithmic tables, opening new and more facile ways of performing calculations, following ideas first published by the Scottish laird John Napier in 1614 and the next years. It was De Decker who, together with his younger friend Adriaen Vlacq, published in 1627 the first complete table of logarithms running from 1–100,000 with base 10; a table computed to 10 decimals. Vlacq had set himself the task of computing the logarithms from 20,000 to 90,000, just as tremendous a deed of computation as van Ceulen's job with the decimals of π, but of greater utility. The other logarithms had already been computed and published, a labor of love performed a few years before by the London professor Henry Briggs, the man after whom the logarithms with base 10 are often called. Briggs had been inspired by Napier himself.

The academic world also took an interest in the art of surveying. In 1613 Willebrord Snel van Royen, known as Willebrord Snellius, became professor of mathematics at the University of Leiden. This important figure in the history of surveying was the son of the first Leiden professor in mathematics, the widely-travelled humanist Rudolf Snel van Royen, already connected with the university since 1578, in his time known as an admirer and editor of books by the Paris mathematician and anti-Aristotelian Petrus Ramus. Rudolf Snel also admired his friend and colleague, the theologian Arminius, like him a native of Oudewater near Gouda, the spiritual leader of those more liberal Calvinists known as Remonstrants during and after the civil strife of 1609—1621. A critical attitude towards Aristotle and the Calvinist doctrine of predestination therefore came to Leiden at an early time.

Willebrord, as a young man an admirer of van Ceulen and Stevin, whose works he translated into Latin, first studied at Leiden, then at Würzburg with Adriaan van Roomen and at Prague with Tycho Brahe and Kepler. His name has remained connected with the law of the refraction of light; the manuscript with this derivation of the law is lost, but was known in the seventeenth century. There is some question whether Descartes saw it before he published the law in his *Principia*. Snellius, the first of the Leiden professors to perform physical experiments, was also a surveyor and carried into practice Gemma Frisius' idea on triangulation − probably the first to do so, though perhaps Blaeu and even van Deventer preceded him with less accurate instruments. He spent many years of his short life (he died in 1626 only forty-six years old) measuring a net of triangles from Alkmaar in the North to Bergen op Zoom in the South and from there, during the truce between the Republic and Spain, as far as Mechelen (Malines). Basis line was the distance from Leiden to the village of Zoeterwoude about four kilometers to the South, a distance he measured again during a winter when the country, flooded and frozen, offered him a beautiful level landscape. The results can be found in the *Eratosthenes batavus* (1617),[11] burdened with errors Snellius could not correct anymore, a task accomplished in the eighteenth century by s'Gravesande. Snellius' estimate of the circumference of the earth amounted to 38,600 kilometers expressed in Rhineland rods.[12] The true length, as we know, is a little more than 40,000 kilometers. In his *Tiphys batavus* (1624), a text on theoretical navigation, he discussed the rhumb lines indicated by Mercator on his world map of 1569 by straight lines. He gave them the name of loxodromes (*loxos*, oblique, *dromos*, course) by which they are known today. Yet we should not take Snellius with all the knowledge he had picked up from Kepler and Stevin and his use of the experimental method as a very modern figure; he believed in the Ptolemaic system, the Aristotelian physics and the forecasting powers of comets. The great break with the past, despite all the work of the great pioneers, came in the Netherlands only with Descartes years after the death of Snellius.

A contribution to this great break also came from two instrument makers living in Middelburg in Zeeland by the name of Zacharias Jansen and his neighbor Hans Lipperhey, the first to bring a telescope, or telescopic spyglass, on the market, maybe primarily for making an honest living. Magnifying lenses had long been known, but Jansen had in 1604 an instrument with a concave ocular (eye lens) and a convex subject lens, made perhaps after an Italian model. In 1608 Lipperhey demonstrated this instrument, still known as the Dutch telescope, to Maurice of Orange and his brother Frederic Henry. He and Jansen were not the only ones to have had the idea; Jacob Metius in Alkmaar, one of the sons of burgomaster Adriaen Anthonisz., had a similar telescope in that same period. The secret was out; it is well known how quickly the news reached Florence, where Galileo constructed an improved version, looked through it to the sky and soon made a series of wonderful discoveries: mountains on the moon, the phases of

Venus, the four "Medici" satellites of Jupiter and the oblong shape of Saturn. Already in 1610 Galileo, in his *Message from the Stars*, his *Sidereus Nuncius*, drew his conclusions from these discoveries: Copernicus was right, the earth is a planet rotating around the sun like the other planets. This, together with the book on the orbit of Mars, published by Kepler in 1609, the *Astronomia Nova*, based on the observations of Tycho Brahe, constituted a powerful support for the still highly unpopular Copernican system. The Copernicans now possessed experimental facts and no longer had to rely exclusively on Platonic and aesthetic speculations. And thus in their own way these instrument makers of Middelburg made their contribution to the later triumph of the heliocentric system.

The telescope was not the only contribution to this victory. Philip van Landsberge(n), native of Ghent, Reformed minister at Goes in Zeeland from 1586 to 1613, and then till his death in 1632 at Middelburg, published in 1619 a plea for the Copernican system, followed in 1629 by a better-known book in Dutch with a similar thesis, translated as *Commentationes in motum terrae diurnum et annuum* (1630) by his pupil Martinus Hortensius, later professor in Amsterdam. This Philip, probably the first Dutch clergyman to openly defend the heliocentric hypothesis, was also the writer of a trigonometry and computed π into 28 decimals (1616) in a way somewhat different from the Archimedean methods used by van Ceulen. In 1663, long after his death, his *Opera omnia* were published, also at Middelburg. We will discuss later Stevin's contribution to the heliocentric system.

There was in these days still another talented craftsman who has made a name for himself, though mainly abroad. Cornelis Drebbel, the "star of 1572", as he has been called, hailed from Alkmaar and, after having shown his inventiveness in his own country by engraving and the construction of better-drawing chimneys, sailed over to England in 1605 where he made a considerable impression at the court of James I with a great display of ingenuity. He also impressed the emperor Rudolph at Prague. Among his noteworthy inventions explosives and a boat that moved under water are mentioned. He must have been a remarkable figure, playing, as is said, with alchemy, with a *perpetuum mobile*, with microscopes, thermostats and with methods to dye tapestry and silk. As so many inventors, he died in poverty (1631); he is often taken as an underestimated genius.

We cannot take leave of our clever mathematicians and instrument makers without mentioning one man who has gained in national fame what he has failed to get on an international scale. We are thinking of Willem Bartjes, schoolteacher, first in Amsterdam. then in Zwolle, the author of a *Cijfferinghe*, first published in 1608, for two centuries with reprints and revisions probably the most popular schooltext on arithmetic in the Netherlands. It was even republished more than once during the nineteenth century. Where the German says Adam Riese and the Englishman says Robert Recorde, the Dutchman says Bartjes, and "according to Bartjes", two times two is still four. Master Willem had literary ambitions and moved in the circle of poets and painters around the Haarlem painter-poet Karel van Mander, author of a well-remembered book on painters after the example of Vasari (1604). Here he also met Holland's greatest poet Joost van den Vondel. He must have impressed the poet as shown by a bit of poetry (1626) that runs somewhat like this:

> Only silence fits the wise,
> While you Bartjes climb the skies.
> Oh, I wish to be on earth
> Just the echo of your worth.[14]

The hosiery merchant apparently recognized his superior in the mathematician.

CHAPTER V

SIMON STEVIN

1

It will be noticed that the majority of these teachers of mathematics and navigation wrote their books in the vernacular, in that stalwart Dutch which Netherlanders even now can appreciate when they read their States Bible, which is for the Dutch what the King James translation is for the English[1], a book written in a language differing so favorably from the horrible semi-French that passed for official language in the Republic. These teachers wanted to talk to those sections of the population ignorant of Latin, in the words of Stevin: "To Astronomers, Land-meters, Measurers of Tapestry, Gaugers, Stereometers in general, Money-Masters and to all Merchants".[2] This was a sign of that healthy democracy that had been so effective in the rebellion against the Spanish grandees and their haughty king. The Republic never was a political democracy, not even in the rather narrow sense in which we usually accept this expression, yet there existed and still exists a strong feeling of sturdy self-consciousness in the hearts and minds of these rebels and sons (and daughters) of rebels in Holland, Zeeland, Frisia and elsewhere, a sentiment notably appearing in Calvinist church communities. The *burghers* spoke Dutch, were proud of it and left Latin to the professors and French to the Court in The Hague. There even were enthusiasts who wanted to elevate the speaking and writing in the mother language to a kind of theory. "All sciences have made the greatest progress when they were explained for all in the daily language of the country", wrote Hugo Grotius, himself a famous Latin scholar. As a young man,

Grotius had looked up with admiration to Stevin, a friend of his father, and he expressed the thoughts of Stevin.

Stevin went far beyond this. He did not only write in Dutch to find a hearing among his neighbors, he also wrote it because he considered it the best language in the world to express one's thoughts, and especially scientific thought. In his *Uytspraek van de Weerdichheyt der Duytsche Tael* (Discourse on the Dignity of the Dutch Language), written as an introduction to his *Weeghconst* (Art of Weighing) of 1586, he presented several proofs to back up his opinions. One was the concise nature of the Dutch language, which he showed by compiling long lists of polysyllabic French and Latin words, expressed in Dutch by only one syllable ('acht, j'estime, existimo', etc.). A well-established Dutch scientific vocabulary did not yet exist and Stevin had to meet the same difficulty which now besets the Israeli, Malayan, Chinese and African peoples, facing the task of translating modern scientific and technical terms into their own idiom. Many expressions of Stevin have been taken over into modern Dutch, sometimes slightly modified, words such as *wiskunde* for mathematics, *driehoek* for triangle, *evenwijdig* for parallel, *evenaar* for equator, *evenredigheid* for proportion. No other Germanic language has gone that far; Kepler's attempts to do something similar for the German language had little succes, and his '*Messkunst*' has remained '*Geometrie*'. M. V. Lomonosov, around 1750, did better for the Russian language.

2

Stevin in origin and education belonged to the same group of self-made men that we have already met in previous chapters and who have had such great merits for the development of the young Republic. He surpassed them in originality, versatility and educational gifts. A native of Brugge in Flanders and, as it seems, trained as a book-keeper, we find him in 1582, at the age of thirty-four, in Leiden where he develops a great productive activity. It is evident that he had studied the leading works in mathematics and mechanics and showed great mastery of their content. Between 1582 and 1586 books from his pen appeared regularly, almost all published by Plantin, first in Antwerp, then in Leiden. The best-known are the *Thiende* (1585), published in English under the title *Disme* in 1608 and the *De Beghinselen der Weeghconst* (Principles of the Art of Weighing) (1586). Other works of this period deal with tables of interest (up to that time usually considered banking secrets), certain difficult geometrical problems inspired by Euclid, Archimedes and Dürer, and an arithmetic and algebra. The algebra is written in a notation that can be considered as a transition between the old clumsy way of writing notations as we still see in Claes Pietersz. or in another form in Cardano, and the modern notation due to Descartes.

De Thiende, a pamphlet of thirty-six pages published in the same year in a French translation entitled *La Disme*, is a plea for the systematic use of the decimal system, especially in the case of fractions. Fractions were usually written with any number as denominator and a kind of dash as in 7/8, or in sexagesimal notation, usually in the following form: $5°6'$ $17''$ $38'''$. Stevin's idea amounts to this. We should operate exclusively with 10 or powers of 10, also in the denominator, to great advantage in the practice of counting, a sound plea in an age where the calculus with fractions was considered something difficult. Stevin wrote our 5.32 in the form of 5 commencements, 3 primes, 2 seconds (actually 5⓪ 3① 2②) or 532 seconds, a notation reminiscent of that used for sexagesimal fractions, and his ideas found a sympathetic audience. In 1616 the Scotsman John Napier,[3] the inventor of the logarithms, accepted Stevin's ideas and suggested a notation with the decimal sign that we still use, to facilitate the use of his logarithmic tables. Stevin's proposition was also given a friendly reception in the Netherlands, in practice by the surveyors Dou and De Decker, and also by Professor van Schooten who introduced it to the academic world. Stevin's suggestion that the decimal system also be adapted to weights and measures was unsuccessful for the time being; its realization only came with the French Revolution and then not even in English-speaking countries. Briggs, in London, attempted to introduce the decimal division also into angle measurement. Keeping the circular quadrant at 90 degrees, he divided the degree into 100 subunits, as can be seen in the *Trigonometria Brittannica* published in 1633 by Vlacq in Gouda. Vlacq, however, did not himself introduce this system in his *Trigonometria artificialis*, published in the same year. In this field the sexagesimal system has been maintained almost everywhere, though we do not subdivide the seconds into tertses, quarts, etc., but decimally, e.g., $5°\ 7'\ 8.5''$ instead of $5°\ 7'\ 8''\ 30'''$. This system is one of the oldest cultural remains preserved in science; it goes back to the Sumerians in Mesopotamia 5,000 years ago.

Stevin's fame with posterity is mainly based on this plea for the general use of decimal fractions; he has influenced its use very strongly indeed. At school we also learn of his sailing chariot,[4] with which he entertained Prince Maurice and his retinue on the beach. This sailing chariot has remained a curiosity even though it inspired around 1850 the Dutch poet Potgieter to a patriotic poem. In the history of mechanics, however, Stevin occupies an important place because of his books on the *Weeghconst* and *Waterwicht* (1586). In this book he was the first to develop systematically the ideas of Archimedes on the equilibrium of solid bodies and liquids. Here we find in the foundations of statics the law of equilibrium of bodies on an inclined plane ('wonder en is gheen wonder'),[5] the law of Archimedes for submerged bodies and the so-called hydrostatic paradox, often ascribed to Pascal in the seventeenth century. Stevin's mathematical reasoning had a sober touch and with his original way of tackling problems that we

now treat with the aid of limits, he influenced the way in which
the principles of Archimedes during the seventeenth century have
passed into the integral calculus. He also checked up on the
Aristotelian theory of motion by an experiment performed together with burgomaster De Groot; they dropped two leaden balls,
one ten times as big as the other, at the same moment from a
height of thirty feet onto a board and discovered that the two
balls fell on the board in such a way that the thump was heard at
the same time. This was "experience against Aristotle" because,
according to him, the heavier ball should have arrived first. This
reminds us of the famous story of Galileo on the leaning tower of
Pisa, but this is placed twenty years later and is probably legend.
The whole way of thinking of Stevin exudes an anti-Aristotelian
spirit in which he was probably encouraged through his constant
contact with engineers and other men of practice, but also by
association with Rudolf Snellius, the admirer of Ramus.

3

We also see Stevin in his role of adviser to the construction of
mills, locks and harbors. He attracted the attention of Prince
Maurice whom he followed into the field and with whom he discussed mathematical and technical questions. It is well known that
Prince Maurice was a clever and famous general, conquering from
the Spanish town after town and defeating them also in the open
field at Nieuwpoort. But Maurice was more than a clever com-
mander. The talented son of a talented father, he belonged to
those military leaders of his time who began to thoroughly understand the great significance of the new sciences for the technique
of warfare. With Maurice we arrive at the beginning of the so-
called scientific art of warfare, in which the mercenary groups of
the past were subjected to the discipline of the developing modern

state. This also led, after its beginning in the Italian Renaissance, to new theories of fortification, a subject on which Stevin also wrote. They grew into a complicated science, paying attention both to mathematical problems and to questions of technique and organization. They replaced the simple wall construction of the Middle Ages by a polygonal structure, a structure calculated to minimize that part of the fortress wall that could not be reached by the defenders with firearms while it tried to make the attack of the enemy as difficult as possible. Friedrich Engels was one of those to point out the great role played in the development of this theory by the German engineer Daniel Speckle. Speckle's ideas, published in 1586, were known to Stevin and to later military engineers such a Menno van Coehoorn under the king-stadhouder William III (who laid out the still existing bastions of Naarden near Amsterdam) and his famous opponent Sébastien de Vauban under Louis XIV. They continued the work of Speckle and Stevin. Don't underestimate the theoretical possibility of this science: the later teachings of Gaspard Monge at the military academy at Mézieres on the Meuse, in the eighteenth century, derived from it what he called descriptive geometry, a science which, together with the more ancient linear perspective, greatly influenced the beginnings of modern geometry. This interest in fortification and architecture also led Stevin to write a book on perspective for Prince Maurice, one of the first theoretical studies in a field developed originally by painters and architects. Stevin was not the only one writing about perspective in the Northern Netherlands; we also have the beautifully illustrated works by the architect Hans Vredeman de Vries, mentioned before, who, after many years of roaming in foreign countries, returned in 1601 to his native country. His ornamental style can still be admired in Amsterdam. Such illustrated books were also published by Stevin's colleague, the military engineer Samuel Marolois, also a writer on fortification. Some of the Dutch painters equally showed loving application of perspective, notably Pieter Saenredam with his church and town pictures. All these beautiful arts and techniques helped to span a bridge between the land of Rembrandt and that of Stevin and Huygens.

Most of Stevin's later works are the result of his association with Maurice. They have been collected in the *Wisconstighe Gedachtenissen*, two stately folios from the years 1605 and 1608. Many writings of Stevin, collected in these tomes, were published at the same time in a Latin translation by Willebrord Snellius and in a partial French translation by a secretary of Prince Frederick Henry, the brother of Maurice. We find here Stevin's books on geometry, perspective, fortification, book-keeping, trigonometry and cosmography. In 1634, after Stevin's death in 1620, almost all his writings were published once more in a French edition prepared by Albert Girard, an engineer from Lorraine with little money and eleven children, who had established himself in Holland. He has another niche in the history of mathematics: in 1629 he gave a first formulation of the so-called fundamental theorem of algebra that states that an algebraic equation has as many roots as its degree indicates. Since this is only true if we admit imaginary numbers, it shows that Girard ventured beyond his admired master, since Stevin, though accepting negative numbers, was allergic to imaginaries.

The cosmography (*'Weereltschrift'*) of Stevin is of some importance since he compares in it Ptolemaic and Copernican world pictures and reaches the conclusion that the Copernican model deserves preference; the earth rotates about its axis and moves about the sun just like the planets (*'Dwaelders'*, Dutch name for rovers or footloose people which is the literal meaning of 'planets'). This was in 1608, before Galileo received his message from the stars and Kepler had published his study of the Martian orbit. Stevin's reasoning had, like that of Copernicus, to be of a rational-aesthetic nature, because no experimental material was available to lend force to the Copernican theory. The ideas of Stevin were, despite the fact that Copernicus' book was already more than sixty years old, about as popular as Marxism is at a present United States university. Many years later Galileo still had to face the Inquisition. In tolerant Holland, with Prince Maurice as his protector, a prince who probably did not care a hoot whether the earth turned around the sun or the sun turned around the earth, Stevin's person was not in danger. But dark clouds gathered on many a theological or professional brow when Stevin's ideas became known. "If these things are true and as I hear, the author defends them tooth and nail, then Moses is a liar, then lies the whole Holy Script. It pains me that the name and the studies of the Prince have been smeared with this tar, the doors and windows have been opened for slander", wrote the learned Emmius in Groningen to the equally learned Lubbertus in Franeker (1608).[6] The debate about the rotation of the earth around the sun would last for decades. The translators of the States Bible adhered strictly to the old interpretation of the Bible text: "Sun, stand thou still upon Gibeon" (Joshua 10:12), and even after 1650 pamphlets appeared pro and contra. This did not prevent the publication in 1637 at Amsterdam of the third edition of Copernicus' book on the Two Systems, even edited by a younger colleague of our friend Emmius, and in 1635 the Regents of Amsterdam appointed a committee to invite Galileo to their city. Nothing, however, came of this initiative.

Stevin never was connected with Leiden University although it tried, from the beginning, to attract the best talents at home and abroad, who did not offend the feelings of Reformed Ministers too much, and although he was friendly with the two Snels, father and son. Was Stevin's limited knowledge of Latin the reason? But he was not even appointed at the Leiden "Dutch" school of engineering, founded in 1600, where Latin was not required − and he lived until 1620. Was it because of his advancing age or perhaps his Copernican heresies? We do not know, though we can very well imagine that the very idea of entrusting the education of the tender minds of the young to such a man must have made the hair of many a good *burgher* stand on end. But we must not believe that Stevin was a rebel. In 1590 he published a booklet called *Het Burgerlijck Leven* (On Civic Life), in which he states that a good subject must arrange his life in accordance with the authorities, and if he gets into circumstances where he finds that one must obey God more than Man, he should not make a public issue out of it, but had better pitch his tents elsewhere, the good American "love it or leave it" thesis. All in all he must have been not only a hard-working and clear-thinking man, but also a pleasant and cheerful chap to whom we can relate with a feeling of friendship through the mist of the ages. We cannot always say the same of the later, enormously clever, but often somewhat grim and unapproachable gentlemen who together have laid the foundation of the great edifice of modern natural science and mathematics.

CHAPTER VI

THE NEW SCIENCE

1

The Republic, that turned clerks into magistrates, skippers into naval heroes, schoolteachers into scholars and painting apprentices into artists also turned the Orange princes, who in their old country probably would never have been more than petty *serenissimi*, into generals and statesmen of the first rank. All have contributed by their intense interest in military technique to the development of those sciences and engineering practices connected with warfare – and the Republic, during the whole Golden Century, knew only a few years of peace. Maurice, of all these princes, achieved much more in this respect than we can conclude from his relation to Stevin alone. He was interested in the University of Leiden where he was a student at the time of his father's assassination, and in 1600 he sponsored, as already mentioned, the "Dutch" engineering school at Leiden with able men as teachers. We also noted his interest in Plancius and scientific navigation in general. Several books dedicated or referring to him bear witness to the respect he enjoyed in scientific circles. He had a reputation of being the ablest general of his time, and men from all parts came to his army to learn the novel art of warfare. True, among those men were plenty of swashbuckling characters of the kind immortalized by Dumas in his *Three Musketeers*, but also serious students like Maurice's youthful relative Johan Maurits, the later "Brazilian", and the young René Descartes.

For many years there existed another court at The Hague beside that of the Oranges. The Elector Frederick of the Palatinate, a

grandson of William the Silent, during a short period King of
Bohemia at the beginning of the Thirty Years' War, fled in 1620 to
the Netherlands and established himself and his large family near
his relatives, the Oranges. This court of the "Winter King", as he
became known, and his wife, the daughter of the English King
James I, must have been a scene of an active intellectual life,
if we may judge from the interest taken by several of Frederick's
eleven children in philosophy and science. One of the sons was
Prince Rupert, a dashing cavalry general under Charles I against
Cromwell, an admiral under Charles II against the United Provinces, a chemist, metallurgist, experimenter with Huygens' pendulum clocks on the British fleet and an inventor of a type of etching
called mezzotint, as well as a kind of brass called Prince Rupert
metal. He was the first governor of the Hudson's Bay Company,
the British fur monopoly in Northern North America, in modified
form still existing in Canada. The whole fur region was once called
Prince Rupert Land. He has even left his mark in mathematics.

Another son of the Winter King, Karl Ludwig, like Rupert a
student at Leiden and Utrecht, recognized as Elector of the
Palatinate after the Peace of Westphalia, was also known for his
interest in learning. He had the courage to offer Spinoza a chair
at his university of Heidelberg, an honor which the philosopher
courteously declined.

And then there were two daughters, Sophia and Elizabeth, who
also made a name for themselves. Sophia married the Elector of
Hannover, became the mother of George I of England and was a
friend of Leibniz. Elizabeth was a pupil and correspondent of
Descartes, to whom the philosopher in 1646 dedicated his treatise
on psychology, called *Passions de l'âme*. She belonged to that
remarkable group of women who lent their grace to the Dutch
Golden Century, women like Anna Roemer Visscher and her sister
Maria Tesselschade, both poets and engravers, Elizabeth of the
Palatinate, the scholarly Anna Maria van Schuurman and, later in

the century, Maria Sibylla Merian, the naturalist. Anna Maria van
Schuurman also appreciated Descartes, but, as a member of the
Utrecht circle around the orthodox Professor Voetius, refused to
reject Calvin for the new philosophy. Later in life, she joined
the religious communist sect of the Labadists. When this sect was
driven from Amsterdam, it found protection with Elizabeth, at
that time (1670) Abbess of the Lutheran *Stift* at Herford in
Westphalia. The Labadists eventually found shelter in a castle near
the village of Wieuwerd in Frisia, where they again attracted remarkable talents. Anna Maria van Schuurman died in that setting.[1]

2

So much for the court aristocracy. Of comparative or even greater
importance was the mercantile class from which, during the early
years of the seventeenth century, a special patrician class developed
as ruling class, we may even say ruling caste, that of the Regents.
Court aristocracy and Regents formed with the Reformed ministers
that remarkable trinity that lent its unique character to the political life of the Republic. There never was much love lost between
the Orange princes and the Regents, so that the *stadhouders* often
leaned on the support of the Reformed preachers in their struggle
with the municipal aristocracy, connected as these preachers were,
generally speaking, with the popular masses and even with the
grauw (the populace, the lower strata of the population). However, there was one area in which Orange princes and Regents
found themselves on the same side and in opposition to leading
orthodox preachers, and that was in their tolerance in matters
of conscience.

One has to be careful with this term, also applicable to Remonstrant preachers, those Arminian preachers who, in one way or
another, reflected the position of the Regents. Practically all

accepted Calvinism and the Dutch Reformed Church, whether they were Plancius or Huygens, Prince Maurice or van Oldenbarnevelt, De Groot or De Witt. When, to paraphrase a Dutch verse of Vondel, "Fighting preachers to their grief — Struggled for the right belief",[2] then it was in both cases the Reformed religion, whether according to the Remonstrant or the Counter-Remonstrant confession. A liberal minister in the present sense of the term would have led an unpleasant life as an atheist, though it must be said that old-fashioned torture or even persecution for religion's sake had more or less gone out of fashion in the seventeenth-century Netherlands. The "latitudinarians", representing the Regent ideal of opposition to what they saw as religious fanaticism, aimed at something like the Anglican church, a state institution with room for Puritans and themselves, united in one confession. The ideal of the orthodox Counter-Remonstrant ministers was a state solidly founded on the Calvinist interpretation of the Bible, a kind of Geneva on the North Sea, a state actually realized by the Puritans of New England — a state grounded in the community of the faithful, not a community of the faithful grounded in the state.

The city aristocracy, mercantile by nature, derived its tolerance primarily from the general principle consciously or unconsciously professed in mercantile activities, that *pecunia non olet*, or, in plain language, that it does not matter whether the pennies reek. This was not only a good principle for the privateers, slave traders and the gentlemen who equipped them, but also for coastal or transit traders who had to deal with all kinds of beliefs and unbeliefs, moralities or immoralities. However, we should not take this in too cynical a vein; the grim period of the religious wars was still fresh in people's memories and, moreover, sectarian division is bad for trade and industry. Thus tolerance in matters of conscience, an "Erasmianism", if not carried too far, became a way of life for many a well-to-do Dutchman and for those who went his way. For the Orange princes this type of tolerance was also in accordance with their politics, which already during William the Silent had become world politics. These politics objected as little to alliances with Pope or Turk as to an occasional kick at the address of Protestant brethren, and the Lord Regents might well give their blessing to it.

This tolerance was beneficial to the cultivation of the sciences. Calvinism, even in its orthodox form such as strict Puritanism, had in principle no objection to it, a subject to which in recent times a good deal of attention has been paid, especially to the relation of Protestantism and science in America and England. It is true that neither Luther nor Zwingli nor Calvin had shown special enthusiasm for all these innovations in the natural sciences or mathematics. They had set themselves another task, the liberation of men's conscience from the Roman tradition. But Rome also stood for Renaissance science, and it was sometimes difficult for a good Protestant not to throw the baby out with the bathwater. In the long run, however, Protestantism, and especially Calvinism, established itself most firmly in those countries where trade, finance and shipping dominated economic life. And when a more capitalist form of economy began to develop in these countries, Protestantism, especially in its Arminian form, also took a more friendly attitude towards the new sciences.

Certain principles in Protestantism were favorable to this attitude. Here was no Inquisition, no index of forbidden books (though many a book or pamphlet in the Republic was prohibited by 'Placaet', i.e., by special order, but not always too strictly enforced). Here was opposition to important features of the medieval world picture and the command that man had to experience the truth in his own conscience. Especially among Calvinists the conviction prevailed that the majesty of God is also revealed in the majesty of nature and that therefore science can contribute to the glorification of the Supreme Being — a conviction somewhat tempered by the thought that the road to God via the study of nature is, after all, somewhat of a detour, and sometimes a dangerous detour, since too much knowledge can bring temptation to man. The fact is, that the Calvinist preachers themselves have achieved very little in the field of the natural sciences or mathematics as compared to the Jesuits and the later Quakers. Their time was probably too much occupied by pastoral duties, penitential sermons and theological disputes. And has not the Preacher already cried out that he who increaseth knowledge, increaseth sorrow? Apart from Plancius and Lansberge, already mentioned, we shall hardly meet these pastors in this book again.[3] We must not forget, however, that the States Bible shows how thoroughly many of them were versed in languages, Dutch as well as Greek, Hebrew and, of course, Latin.

The carriers of the exact sciences in the first period of the Republic were, as we have seen, more or less well-to-do, but hard-working and industrious *burghers*, school-teachers, pilots, surveyors, instrument makers and engineers, a type exemplified by Stevin and also represented by the painters of that period. In the later years of the Eighty Year War, the city aristocrats become prominent as a ruling class, dominated by aristocratic families in Amsterdam. In the formative years of the Regent State and during the years when it was ruled by powerful figures like Jan De Witt, the city aristocrats also took over the leadership in the sciences. The Regents and those who more or less shared their class position, tolerant in religion, receptive to unorthodox ideas, encouraged the new scientific currents as well as the new philosophy. Directly or indirectly, they drank from the Cartesian well. The science of the second period of the Golden Century had, generally speaking, a somewhat aristocratic character and is represented by Huygens. After all, people of social standing were best equipped to withstand the attacks of the anti-Cartesian, often Counter-Remonstrant, parsons. When, at the end of the seventeenth century, the Regent state begins to show signs of regression, we also find a shift of the point of gravity in scientific research. Swammerdam and Leeuwenhoek were certainly no members of the Regent class; Swammerdam even got himself into some kind of opposition.

3

The interest of the rich merchants, of the Lord Regents, in science and technology had a material foundation. As tolerant in matters of the spirit as intolerant in matters of commercial competition, they did not only have the money to entertain themselves with the arts and sciences, but also to invest in them. The profits in mercantile activity, piracy, slave trade and colonial exploitation, especially those of the East India Company founded in 1602, were so large that not all the available capital could be invested easily and safely, not even with all fleets equipped. Dignified houses with art collections and libraries, with the beautiful books published by Plantin, Elzevier or Blaeu constituted one form of investment. The famous girdle of canals around the ancient center of Amsterdam, flanked by aristocratic dwellings in Renaissance style (Herengracht, Keizersgracht, Prinsengracht) was laid out in the years after 1612. There were 'rariteitenkabinetten', collections of curiosities, private museums, conducive to the study of natural history, as well as the 'lustwarandes', botanical gardens, pleasances outside the city walls around charming country mansions, often near a winding river or watercourse. With the population growing, a favorite form of investment was the drainage of lakes and estuaries. This was as beneficial to the Dutch science of engineering as was the military engineering of the Orange princes with their sieges and fortifications.

The tradition was of long standing; drainage of lakes or parts

of the sea and dike-building was not unknown to the Middle Ages
and the Burgundian-Habsburg time so that considerable technical
expertise was available.[4] Dutch drainage engineers were famous far
and wide. Among the patricians who invested their money in such
often speculative enterprises we find members of the Zeeland
family Cats, well known in the Netherlands, because one of them,
Jacob Cats, pensionary (attorney general) of the states of Holland
and West Frisia from 1636 to 1651, has for centuries, as 'Father
Cats', been the beloved Dutch poet of domestic virtue and wisdom
(with seventeenth-century frankness). The best-known drainage
expert of this period was Jan Adriaansz. Leeghwater. Born in De
Rijp in the middle of the lakes and waterways north of Amsterdam,
the result of inundation and the digging of peat for centuries,
Leeghwater contributed greatly to their drainage. He knew how to
master the improving windmill technique, also studied by Stevin,
and applied it to the *inpoldering* (drainage) of the Beemster (1608
–1612 with 41 windmills, 18,000 acres), Purmer (1618–1622,
6,800 acres) and Wormer (1624–1626, 4,000 acres). In his
Haerlemmermeerboek (Haarlem Lake Book) (1641), he also
proposed a plan for draining the huge and, in stormy weather,
very dangerous Haarlem Lake (45,000 acres), but the execution
had to wait until 1848–1852 when steam engines were used. One
of them is called after Leeghwater, another after an eighteenth-
century engineer, Nicolaas Kruik or Cruquius, now a museum.
Amsterdam's airport Schiphol is built inside the *polder* of the
former Haarlem Lake.

Leeghwater's skills[5] were also appreciated in France, Lorraine
and Holstein. But the engineer who became most famous abroad
was Vermuyden, also from Zeeland. After having made his name
by *inpolderingen* in his own country, working among others for
the Cats family, he was invited by James I to drain a swampy
area in East Anglia that belonged to the Crown. It seems that he
used no mills, but achieved the drainage by diverting waterways,

digging the ditches that still characterize the Fens between Ely and the Wash. Vermuyden gained and lost a fortune in the work of draining these marshlands, his financial relations with James I and Charles I involving him in the politics of the British revolution; but whatever his fate, he could boast of a beautiful title: Sir Cornelius Vermuyden. The Southern Netherlands also participated in the drainage enthusiasm. Here the supervising genius was the many-sided Wenzel Cobergher, painter, architect, antiquarian, chemist and engineer, best known as the Renaissance man who introduced the Baroque style into present Belgium. In the year 1622 and after he supervised the drainage of the 8,000-acre swampy tract called De Moeren near Veurne in West Flanders, using drainage moats and windmills, one of which is still alive.[6]

Another form of investment were the industries, old and new. New life was breathed into the textile industry of Leiden, already known in the Middle Ages. Tapestry weavers, sugar refiners, glass blowers, lace workers, porcelain makers, potters and brewers lent a good name to Dutch manufacture on the world market. Many of these industries introduced new inventions. Shipbuilding was known of old. Amsterdam got its first fire engine with suction pumps in 1657. The flourishing clay pipe industry of Gouda was started around 1620 by English religious refugees. Dutch instrument making was highly developed, witness the beautiful "Frisian" and "Dutch" clocks ("grandfather clocks") that grace the living rooms and museums. The brothers Hemony, François and Pierre, from Lorraine, were and still are famous as bell casters.

And then there were the windmills. The earliest of them mentioned in the Netherlands date from the thirteenth century and were used for grinding grain. In the fifteenth century drainage mills are mentioned. But the great flowering of the windmills came with the Republic. Dutch inventiveness found evermore new applications: mills for sawing timber, the hulling of rice, fulling, the crushing of oil seeds, the grinding of pigments, snuff, mustard, cinnamon mills, papermills. Everywhere, but especially in the open watery region of the river Zaan, just north of Amsterdam, the mills were merrily turning in the freely blowing wind. Almost every town had one or more windmills on its bastions. The United Provinces in the eighteenth century must have had some 8,000 wind mills, each characterized by its own technical name (*wipmolen, buitenkruier, binnenkruier, paltrokmolen*, etc.). There were also watermills, by which term we do not mean windmills used for drainage, but mills with a wheel on a stream. Examples were the papermills on the East border of the sandy forest and heathlands of the Veluwe in Gelderland, on rivulets often artificially laid out. The oldest mill was in Arnhem, built in 1591. Many of these mills were in the neighborhood of Apeldoorn. In 1740 there were 171 water-papermills and two wind-papermills, and small industries worked by a few men.[7] Paper was made from rags.

All this activity meant the use of ancient and experimentation with new industrial production methods with discoveries and inventions. This development must not only have influenced the arts of glass blowing and ceramics, but also the art of painting, a subject to which, if we are not mistaken, as little attention has been paid as to the whole of Dutch technology and craftsmanship of the Golden Age.

Some of these trades were domestic industries which had barely outgrown ancient guilds. Others were already capitalistically organized with employers and wage labor, shareholders, dividends, the forming of surplus value and, here and there, already the division of labor. We mentioned clocks; the manufacture of these instruments can be taken as typical for this economic period. William Petty, the seventeenth-century English economist, quoted this industry as an example of artful composition from many parts. The clock made a deep impression, not only on mathematicians, but also on philosophers, especially of the Cartesian school, who did not cease to compare the mechanism of the clock with the function of the universe, seeing God as an exquisite craftsman. Apart from its use as a time piece and an example for the mechanical structure of the world, it also played an important psychological role. It taught men to live by the clock, to set exact times for appointments and work hours so as to understand that "time is money". In the precapitalist period, men's behavior was usually controlled by the sun; even the hour glass only appeared in the Middle Ages.

Manufacture, this first stage of capitalism, therefore had an important, if only secondary role in the Republic, and we can therefore talk not only of a commercial aristocracy, but of a capitalist class, a class which also was able to obtain profits from the exploitation of the colonies and eventually also of colonial plantations.

Capitalism does not only mean surplus value, but also invention, discovery, technology and science on a larger scale than before. With it appears an intellectual climate that we might call the capitalist spirit. By this we mean more than the commercial spirit or the desire for profits alone: this was also in the mind of the Phoenicians, the Romans and the picturesque traders in *One Thousand and One Nights*. The commercial spirit alone leads in the sciences to counting with a transition to algebra, to a practical geometry or mensuration, to descriptive astronomy, enough geography and cartography to undertake large voyages and interest in plants, animals and minerals especially from a utilitarian point of view. The capitalist spirit transcends this by far. It brings the desire to understand nature and force it into service to men, the strong desire for better inventions, for more and deeper science; in the first place to use this knowledge to make profits, but also far beyond this as an abstract desire, as a tremendous passion to know and to understand. *Felix qui potuit rerum cognoscere causas* — happy are they who understand the causes of things — was said by the poet Virgil who had been under the influence of Epicurus, whose theory found more and more attention in the seventeenth century. The great poet Lucretius, pupil of Epicurus, was published in Holland more than once.[8]

With the capitalistically minded *burghers* and in other countries with the half-feudal elements financially connected with them, there was, therefore, a growing desire to find a philosophy rationalistically inclined towards nature, averse to the supernatural and the occult, and, therefore, offering greater opportunity than ever for discoveries in nature and inventions in technology. So long as commerce preceded manufacture as the source of profit, and this was typical for the mercantilist period, stress toward innovation was on science as such rather than on its application to industrial technology. Let it be understood: in all ages man has longed for understanding the essence of nature, often through religion and magic, but only with the development of capitalism the systematic desire for a philosophy that served not only to explain, but also to control nature became typical of the ruling class, or at any rate of the most conscious section of such a class. Such an insight would not only lead, as before, to clever toys, but also to instruments, tools and machines. For some of the best representatives of human thought in those days the desire to come to such a philosophy took the form of a desire to make life of mankind easier through science and technology, but the ruling classes as a whole were very little or not at all interested in this approach; in practice, only a small section of the population remained to enjoy the full advantage of the new science. Even in the nineteenth century, John Stuart Mill, the English economist and philosopher, could state that it is questionable if all the mechanical inventions yet made had lightened the daily toil of any human being – a statement which Marx corrected by saying "of any human being not fed by other people's labor". However, the attempt to understand and control nature by reason and experiment has remained typical of all phases of capitalism, even of the period of its decay, even though it has never been able to free itself from obscurantist and even anti-human elements — as we can see today only too clearly.

4

In the formative years of capitalism, the time called by Marx that of primitive accumulation, there was no outlook on the world that gave full inspiration to those who wanted to understand and control nature. Neither the Aristotelian or the Platonic philosophy, nor the Christian, Jewish, or Islamic theologies could help this rationalistic program, enriched by the results of the new science and technology, to a lasting foundation. There were elements of importance in these doctrines, as the admiration of Platonism for mathematics and quantity in general, the Aristotelian studies of logic and of the living world, the Epicurean doctrine of atoms, the Thomists' stress on the possibility to understand the outside world with the aid of reason. But the unity of the world outlook was shattered. Before, however, a new outlook on nature could be construed, it was necessary to come to an agreement on a method that could indicate the new position and clarify the possibility of a constant rational development, with the Church if possible, against the Church if necessary. Already Ramus, around 1560, was talking about it, though primarily as a pedagogical-logical precept. Towards the beginning of the seventeenth century, confidence in the power of the new sciences and technology had grown sufficiently to make a discussion of such a general method a much more encompassing enterprise than Ramus had in mind. A class existed that could encourage the new prophets, and they actually did appear. The best-known of them are the Italian Galileo Galilei, the Englishman Francis Bacon and the Frenchman René Descartes.

Among these three Galileo, a university professor in Padua, later astronomer of the Medici in Florence, concentrated most on the development of a special new science — modern mechanics. He based his science on the theory of falling bodies and derived the law of proportionality of paths and the squares of the times. Galileo's contribution was, strictly speaking, kinematics, i.e., the theory of motion; the theory of forces, or dynamics, was only seriously taken up by his successors, such as Huygens in Holland. Galileo also extended his investigations to the stars, where he provided the Copernican system with new proofs, now based on observation. Galileo understood that mechanics could only lead to control of the phenomena if it is based on mathematics, so that mathematical treatment became, for him, the foundation of the new conception of the world: a revolutionary break with Aristotle. The book of nature, wrote Galileo, is written in mathematical language, the letters are triangles, circles and other geometrical figures, without which it is humanly impossible to understand a single word. The absolute unchanging primary properties of the objectively existing things can only be expressed in mathematical or mechanical terms, properties such as form, magnitude, place, relative position, and condition of motion. Color, taste, odor, degree of heat are secondary properties; they do not exist in the things themselves but express our perceptions. Galileo rejects the argument from authority and recognizes systematic reasoning with the use of mathematical methods as the source of true knowledge. These ideas can already be found in Kepler, but still colored by a religious mysticism, inspired by both Christianity and Platonism. Galileo's writings lack this mysticism; there is, in his way of reasoning, much that reminds us of his older contemporary Stevin.

Francis Bacon, English aristocrat and chancellor of James I, "Verulanus" as he was called, concentrated his attention on that side of the New Method that exists in the necessity of experiment for human welfare. No idle speculation, he declared in his *Novum Organum* (1620), but rather conclusions based on direct experience can bring us mastery over nature. Torment nature, he wrote, to betray its secrets, and so he composed programs of possible experimentation to provide the sciences with that necessary experimental material they need to become more than idle prattle. He also analyzed the so-called idols, the different forms in which men can be lead into error. Bacon had an aversion to mathematics as an aid to find the truth in nature and did not advance a single special science, but his eloquent pleas (all three men, Galileo, Bacon, Descartes, were masters of the written word) for systematic experimental research, for the so-called inductive method, had great effect on later scientists. When in 1662, in England, the Royal Society was founded to encourage such investigations, the great importance of Bacon, already dead for many years, was explicitly recognized. Bacon, more than his leading contemporaries, emphasized that the promotion of the sciences had to aim at the improvement of man's fate — even though, as we fear, in his view man only started where the merchant begins. He can also be considered the pioneer of industrial science. Bacon was a little worried that all this experimenting would give unscrupulous men the opportunity to make more and meaner instruments of destruction. He only hoped that religion would be able to frustrate these designs.

Neither Bacon nor Galileo had much to do with the Republic. We can be certain that the statesman Bacon, as so many of his English contemporaries, paid great attention to the flowering of the United Provinces. Galileo had some contact with the Netherlands in connection with the burning problem of finding the longitude at sea. He presented his new method to the States General in 1635, a method based on the eclipses of the four moons of Jupiter he had discovered. These eclipses, if tabulated, would because of their frequent occurrence be able to provide that celestial clock impossible to obtain from lunar and solar eclipses with their relative rarity. The States General were courteous and Galileo was even, as we shall see, invited and offered a prize; but Galileo did not come and the prize does not seem to have reached him. His method really was of great use on land after 1668, when Jean Dominique Cassini, then at Bologna, published eclipse tables for these Jupiter moons and also enriched astronomy in many other respects. Olaus Römer, working with Cassini at the newly founded Paris observatory, discovered in 1675, by the observation of these eclipses, that light had a finite velocity. Huygens, who in those days was associated with the Paris Academy and its observatory, saw his own work on pendulum clocks intimately related to this astronomical research. Galileo's method, even with Cassini's tables, never had any success on the rolling and pitching seacastles gracing the oceans at the time of the Dutch naval heroes, because even the ablest pilots were unable to observe those eclipses through their spyglasses. Moreover, few had the mathematical training necessary for this determination of longitude.

It is worth mentioning that Galileo's book of 1638, the *Nuove Scienze*, in which he introduced in the form of a dialogue the principles of the new science of mechanics, appeared in Leiden with Elzevier. We mentioned already, that the third edition of Galileo's book on the *Due Sistemi del Mondo* had appeared in Amsterdam in 1637.

Simon Stevin (1548–1620) (*Bibliotheek der Rijksuniversiteit, Leiden*).

BEGHINSELEN
DER WEEGHCONST
BESCHREVEN DVER
SIMON STEVIN
van Brugghe.

TOT LEYDEN,
Inde Druckerye van Christoffel Plantijn,
By Françoys van Raphelinghen.
cIɔ. Iɔ. LXXXVI.

Title Page of *The Art of Weighing* by Stevin (1586) (*Museum Boerhaave, Leiden*).

Paper Mill, brought over to the Open Air Museum, Arnhem (*Rijksmuseum voor Volkskunde, Arnhem*).

Water mill at Wijk-bij-Duurstede (1659) near the river Lek (© *Fotobureau Agtmaal*).

Réné Descartes (1596−1650), after a painting by Frans Hals in the Louvre, Paris.

MATH. PRACTICAE PROFESS. IN LINGUA VERNACULA. CIƆIƆCLVII. OBIIT CIƆIƆCLX.

Frans van Schooten Junior (1615–1660) (*Bibliotheek der Rijksuniversiteit, Leiden*).

Christiaan Huygens (1629–1695). Copper engraving by G. Edelinck (*Museum Boerhaave, Leiden*).

The "Hofwijck" near The Hague – the last home of Huygens (*Huygens Museum, "Hofwijck", Voorburg.* © *Polyvisie, Hilversum*).

CHAPTER VII

DESCARTES

1

What the Republic missed in personal contact with Bacon and Galileo was amply compensated by the presence of Descartes. The twenty years that the French philosopher spent in the Republic belong to the most productive of his life. He came to the Northern Netherlands because its relative tolerance made it easier than elsewhere for him to talk, to write and to publish, and also, it seems, to maintain a little distance between himself and those friends likely to interfere too much with his meditations. René Descartes, Latinized Renatus Cartesius, was born in 1596 near Tours, son of a lawyer with relations to the nobility and the wealthier middle class, a member of the *noblesse de robe*. René received his education at the Jesuit college of La Flèche at Anjou, founded in 1609 by Henry IV as a model for the sons of noble families. The Jesuit order, founded in 1540, consisted of militant champions of the Counter-Reformation dedicated to the preservation of the old faith against Protestantism in a mercantilist society on its way to capitalism. They concentrated on missionary and educational work and aspired to the mastery of the new science without a new method, but inside the framework of the traditional Aristotelian-Thomistic system. We leave it open here whether or not they succeeded in this, but the Jesuits, especially during the sixteenth and seventeenth centuries, have given us excellent mathematicians and astronomers. Although they themselves had some difficulty in coming to Holland, their writings were read. Stevin had admiration for Father Clavius, the astronomer of the Vatican, prime mover of

the Gregorian calendar reform, and we also know that young
Huygens studied the mathematics of the Antwerp Jesuit Grégoire
de Saint Vincent, not without giving him a hard nut to crack with
regard to the quadrature of the circle. Descartes always endeavored
to preserve his friendship with the Catholic authorities and to con-
vince them that his principles were in harmony with the Catholic
faith.

But Descartes was rather disappointed with what he had learned
at La Flèche. He found the stuff dark or sterile. He only had
respect for the mathematics, and when he began to think independently — we are in the beginning of the seventeenth century
when such thinking was encouraged in influential circles — he took
mathematics as an example of that clarity, of those *jugements
clairs et distincts*, that he wanted to see introduced also into
further thought. Descartes, who had visited the Republic in 1617
and in 1621–1622, returned in 1629 and remained there, not for
a long time at one place, but long enough to understand Dutch.
Here he developed his philosophy and science, published his books
and maintained his large correspondence. Frans Hals has painted
his portrait, a realistic representation of this rather stern gentleman who proposed a philosophy of nature in which, in a certain
sense, we still live despite all change. His philosophy as a whole
was dualistic, half idealistic as to the soul (to save religion), half
materialistic with respect to nature (to save science). We are interested in his materialistic theory of nature; departing from doubt,
Descartes first found security in God and through Him in the
possibility of obtaining true knowledge such as offered in mathematics. From this mathematical foundation he continued to
develop his thought that men, with the aid of reason supported
by observation and experiment, can obtain true knowledge of
nature and its laws. And this not only directly through reason and
the senses, but also by means of instruments such as these optical
glasses with which Galileo had seen mountains on the moon and

spots on the sun. This knowledge, continued Descartes, is obtained by the understanding that matter is subjected to the laws of mechanics and these laws are of a mathematical nature. Matter itself was determined mathematically as something which had extension. To us this sounds perhaps rather obvious, except that for us matter is more than extension, and the laws of nature are more than mechanics alone. This rejection in science of belief in authority, tradition or revelation, this use of mathematical reasoning in the formulation of natural laws, this reliance on experiment, is exactly what we learned in school. But this does not prove that Descartes was just producing superficial prattle, but it shows how much these Cartesian thoughts still dominate all our research and education in the natural sciences. In the seventeenth century, when Descartes published his ideas, they were so little obvious that they met with great resistance. This resistance was very strong in the Republic among some Counter-Remonstrant theologians, especially at the University of Utrecht under the leadership of the learned Gijsbert Voet, or Voetius as he used to call himself. Already the fact that Descartes started from doubt instead of revelation was blasphemy in many a religious eye. At Leiden, despite its reputation of open-mindedness in the arts and sciences, philosophical debates ran so high that authorities more than once prohibited the discussion of Cartesian doctrines. Among the leading patricians, scientists and physicians Cartesianism was, as a rule, well received and eventually greatly admired. Here, in principle, they were presented with the key to a satisfying conception of the world able to replace Aristotelianism and to accomplish what the latter could not achieve: to explain the behavior of matter and thus promote science and inventions without being bothered by the prestige of ancient authority. We can say that only by ca. 1680 the often bitter debates came to an end, together with the debates on Copernicus. Even the sharp edge in the theological debates was blunted.

The first publication of Descartes' ideas was in the *Discours de la Méthode pour bien conduire sa raison et de chercher la vérité dans les sciences* (Discourse on the Method of Properly Conducting One's Reason and of Seeking the Truth in the Sciences) of 1637, in a nicely and anonymously published edition by Jean Le Maire in Leiden (Elzevier should have been the publisher, but had made objections). The title already tells us that the booklet sketches a program, a method. It is typical that it is not written in Latin but in French; like Galileo and Stevin, these men wanted to speak above all to their own countrymen, like Galileo in Italian, Stevin in Dutch. To this exposition of his method Descartes added as illustration three essays − one on geometry, one on meteors and one on dioptrics, i.e., the theory of the refraction of light. In the last essay we find the well-known law of refraction already found by Snellius (and, as we now know, also by the Englishman Thomas Hariot) and here published for the first time. The essay on geometry called *La Géométrie* opened a new period in the history of mathematics.

The new kind of mathematics, introduced by Descartes, was the application of Renaissance algebra to the geometry of the Greeks. The coordinate method thus introduced has now entirely been absorbed by our analytical geometry and calculus. This was a practical example of how new ways could be discovered to control nature mathematically, since the new geometry could again be of help to penetrate deeper into mechanics, astronomy and natural science in general. In this way mathematics turned from being a hobby of schoolteachers, pilots and surveyors into the principal tool of the philosopher − a Platonic idea with which Kepler and Galileo had already toyed, but that now received philosophical sanction by Descartes. More than ever mathematics became the Queen of the Sciences.

Already at an earlier date Descartes had begun to write down his ideas. His meditations were in their first form put on paper in

1628 when he was in France, after which he began to write his
cosmology, a treatise to encompass his picture of the world.
Among the important events that influenced his thinking was the
discovery of the circulation of the blood by William Harvey,
published in 1628, as well as the appearance of Galileo's *Dialogue
on the Two World Systems* of 1632, that lively defence of the
Copernican system. These were great events: attacks on Galen, on
Ptolemy, on Aristotle, still highly esteemed masters in many an
academic and professional circle. Reaction was due to come, and
the condemnation of Galileo by the inquisition in 1633 had to
make Descartes, a good son of the Catholic Church, rather careful.
It was possible for him to openly appreciate Harvey's doctrine in
which the heart was introduced as a pump and that thus could
contribute to Descartes' mechanical interpretation of the body's
behavior; moreover, Harvey's method, experimental and quantitative, was entirely in support of the new method, in the sense of
Bacon as well as in that of Descartes. However, as to the Copernican doctrine Descartes, who was inclined towards its acceptance,
was prudent enough not to publish his cosmology. Later he
elaborated his ideas in the *Meditationes* of 1641 and the *Principia
philosophiae* of 1644, Latin books of which editions appeared
with Elzevier, just as his already mentioned French book on the
passions that appeared in 1650, the year in which Descartes died
in Stockholm. He also laid down his thoughts in an extensive
correspondence.

Starting from his method, Descartes by and by came to something which began to look more like a system and appeared to
many people as a structure of metaphysical, dogmatic character.
With admiration, yes rapture, some of his pupils saw how the great
man, starting from simple principles, prepared the whole of nature
for mechanical interpretation, starting from reason alone (from
time to time aided by experiment), including even the animals
whom he took for machines. This is due to the fact, Marx says,

that Descartes looked at animals with the eye of the period of manufacture as objects, in contrast to the outlook of the Middle Ages which looked at an animal like a dog or horse as an aid to man. But we have to be somewhat cautious with the so-called dogmatism of Descartes. He did understand the value of experimentation, and for years had a mechanic in his service. Though he was not particularly inclined to praise others, he wrote with great sympathy about Bacon – "Verulanus" – the apostle of the inductive method. We thus also have to be a little careful with respect to the often proclaimed thesis that there were two principal directions in seventeenth-century natural philosophy, an inductive one represented by Bacon and a deductive one represented by Descartes. The New Method took many forms, elucidated by the different writers in their own special way, but there was also a certain unity in the rationalist method of these seventeenth-century scientists of the period of the ascending *burgher* class, as there is in the dialectical method of the nineteenth- and twentieth-century leaders of the socialist movement. The mathematical deductive method of Newton is after all a direct product of Bacon's school and the great development of the so-called experimental philosophy in the later years of the seventeenth and first half of the eighteenth century, also in the Republic, took place among those who had passed through the school of Descartes. Deduction and induction both play a leading role in modern natural science and, in the seventeenth century, we already find in Huygens a master representing both directions.

2

When Descartes came in 1617 as a young man to the Netherlands to play the soldier under Maurice, he made in Breda the acquaintance of the physician Isaac Beeckman, a native of Middelburg, ten years his senior and at that time teaching at the Latin school of Veere and soon afterwards at that of Utrecht. They met in connection with one of those publicly posted arithmetical problems, by means of which the mathematics teachers of that time used to get the better of each other. Descartes and Beeckman became friendly and discovered that they were interested in more sophisticated problems than the solving of little mathematical puzzles. In 1618 they collaborated in the study of the motion of falling bodies, at the time in which also Galileo was engaged in his meditations on this subject. The result was the oldest known attempt to connect the behavior of falling bodies with the action of gravity, hence a dynamical, not a kinematical, consideration. In the notes of Beeckman, his *Journael*, not published until this century, we find the proportionality of the path traversed with the square of the time, a result that Galileo published independently in 1638 (in his already mentioned *Nuove Scienze*). These notes of Beeckman contain much more, such as statements as "what once moves, continues to move, if it is not interfered with," that show some understanding of the law of inertia, a law that during the seventeenth century would replace the Aristotelian theory of motion. In the theory of inertia, up to the present day the foundation of our mechanics, a uniform rectilinear motion remains invariant unless there is an external force working on the body, where Aristotle, as we have seen, claimed that every motion has to be maintained with external help (except the so-called natural one and those of the celestial spheres). We also find in Beeckman's *Journael* much about the theory of music, a subject of interest to mathematicians ever since antiquity, and also much of a personal nature.

Beeckman remained in contact with Descartes, though their relationship later cooled off a little. After teaching in Utrecht and then in Rotterdam he became rector of the Latin school in Dordrecht from 1627 until his death in 1637, where he had among

his pupils the later so famous Jan and Cornelis De Witt, sons of
one of the burgomasters. He also corresponded with many leading
mathematicians and philosophers of his time, establishing personal
contact with such men as Father Mersenne,[1] the Paris Franciscan,
center of international scientific correspondence till his death in
1648, and Gassendi, another French clergyman who sought, in
opposition to Descartes, to reestablish the validity of the ancient
atom doctrine of Democritus and Epicurus. In this exchange of
opinions the usual topics were mechanics, optics and music.
Beeckman never became as famous as Galileo or Descartes –
though some writers mention the three in one breath – and this
mainly because he was not interested in publicity, kept his ideas
to himself and at most presented them in a letter or in conversa-
tion. After his death his *Meditationes* were published by his
brother (1644). The *Journael* to which Beeckman confided his
ideas remained in manuscript kept in a Middelburg archive, until
it was rediscovered in 1905 by the historian C. de Waard. Now it
has been published and edited in four big volumes (1939–1953),
so that, taking some trouble, we now can appreciate the riches of
Beeckman's spirit in his own words, Dutch and Latin.

Beeckman's formulation of the concept of inertia is still rather
vague because it can be interpreted in such a way that, for instance,
the body moving in a circle will continue to move in a circle without external interference, a concept that even Galileo never quite
abandoned. A more satisfying statement is found in Descartes'
Principia philosophiae of 1644, where he explains his laws of
motion, and where we find that all bodies moving in a straight line
will continue in that motion unless there is an external cause. This
is one of the statements in which Descartes has been confirmed in
his scientific work; most of his special theorems or theories were
outdated soon after his death.

There is one field, however, where his star is as bright as ever, and
that is mathematics. Here we meet Professor Frans van Schooten

in Leiden, who more than anybody else in Holland made Cartesian mathematics known and appreciated. The grandson of a Leiden baker, who emigrated from Flanders, and the son of another Frans van Schooten who succeeded van Ceulen in 1611 as a teacher of mathematics at the Leiden school of engineering, he had been able to study at the university in that city. In 1635, at the age of twenty, he took over his father's lectures in "Dutch mathematics" at the school. It seems that the family had an artistic touch — Joris, the brother of the older Frans, painted portraits of local militia groups — and the younger Frans drew in 1636 the figures for the two appendices on meteors and light published by Descartes during the next year in his *Discours de la méthode*. After traveling for several years in England and France he succeeded his father in 1646 as a teacher at the engineering school, a position he held until his death in 1660 at the age of forty-five.

Van Schooten remained active in the Cartesian camp, he drew the figures for the *Principia*, was in contact with Elizabeth of the Palatinate and translated Descartes' *Géométrie* into Latin. He was also the editor of the collected works of the French mathematician Viète, a contemporary of Stevin, whose algebraic discoveries were so fertile for Cartesian geometry. But van Schooten's greatest influence on the world of science was through his pupils, either at school or in private. Among them we find Jan De Witt, Johannes Hudde, later magistrates, van Heuraet who died young but made a name for himself in the prehistory of the calculus, and above all Christiaan Huygens. In 1659 van Schooten published a new edition of the Latin translation of Descartes' *Géométrie* and here he also collected, with his own commentary, some important investigations into Cartesian geometry by his pupils, such as the contribution by Hudde and by van Heuraet to what we now call the calculus. A few years earlier, in a book which contained some of his own investigations, he had in the same manner presented the young Huygens to the scientific world. Huygens' contribution was nothing more or less than the announcement of a new science — the mathematical theory of probability, or as he called it, the computation of games of chance, *ludi aleae*.

Among those who studied the ideas of Descartes we have met the patrician and Regent *par excellence*, grand pensionary Jan De Witt, a pupil of Beeckman from the time of his early youth in Dordrecht, and pupil of van Schooten in Leiden. This extraordinary man of great versatility and extraordinary energy, the Republic's leading statesman for many years, also found time in his busy life to ponder mathematical problems. From his books on plane curves, published in 1650 and 1661, we can see that he was able to apply both the classical Greek methods of Apollonius and the new algebraic methods of Cartesius — books of sufficient interest to have been made the subject of special study in recent years. And this is not all, De Witt is also one of the pioneers of the mathematics of life insurance. In 1671, shortly before his untimely death, he wrote a *Waerdije van Lijfrenten* (Evaluation of Annuities) in response to a proposition to pay such annuities submitted to the States of Holland and West Frisia. The *Waerdije* contains a method of computation for buying annuities which contain the elements of an exact method. In the computation De Witt was assisted by Hudde and others. Hudde, for many years burgomaster of Amsterdam, is likewise an interesting figure who, despite his many activities as a Regent, found time for scientific work, not only in mathematics and statistics but also in microscopy. With Huygens, in 1671, he also made a study on the improvement of the water supply in the Ysel, a Rhine arm in Gelderland. Hudde's younger colleague as burgomaster of Amsterdam, the merchant-patrician Nicolaas Witsen, also deserves our attention. A man of many parts like Hudde, geographer, cartographer, engraver, hydraulic expert, even orientalist, the author of a book on shipbuilding (1672) and another one on 'Tartarije'

(1692), written after travels to Russia, he was the logical host to Czar Peter the Great when he came to Holland in 1697–1698 to study shipbuilding. As one of the Lords Seventeen, he is also credited with the introduction of coffee production into Java. He lived until well into the eighteenth century.

Let us return to the statistical investigations of De Witt and Hudde at a time that there was also interest in such work in neighboring countries. Economically they are a consequence of the consolidation of the Regent state which led to a more scientific treatment of public finances, a phenomenon that we also find in other countries under the mercantilist system.[2] From a philosophical point of view these investigations are under the influence of the Cartesian mathematization of science, a trend that we can also connect with mercantilism. Around the same time William Petty did related work in England; we already referred to his political arithmetic. In this idea that the method of mathematics could be applied to all kinds of subjects apart from astronomy and mechanics, the origin of statistics can be seen and, to a certain extent, the whole of that newly developing science, political economy. Huygens demonstrated that even such a phenomenon of the world as chance, which did not in the least seem to be of a mathematical nature, but rather belonged to the domain of God, could be subjected to mathematical laws, and now De Witt showed how life expectancy could be studied in a similar way. In the Cartesian school the idea began to gain ground that only mathematics could give a satisfactory character to science as a whole and even to philosophy. Spinoza first formulated the philosophy of Descartes and later his own philosophy in a geometrical form, and Leibniz applied mathematics to Aristotelian logic with results that have been appreciated only in the present time. Less profound persons began to foster a kind of superstition in the power of the mathematical method. There is still something of this left in the world, though few persons will

go as far as that honest theologian/mathematician in early nineteenth century America who applied the laws of Galileo to the
story of falling angels and thus found that hell has a depth of
1,832,308,362 miles.[3]

CHAPTER VIII

CHRISTIAAN HUYGENS

1

Christiaan was the son of the Hague patrician Constantijn Huygens, friend and admirer of Descartes, secretary to the Orange princes, diplomat, man of letters, lover of music and composer, friend of the sciences, a wit, or as the French say, a *bel esprit*, and a man of great vitality, whose poetry, concise and often epigrammatic, is still part of the Dutch high school curriculum. In the Netherlands the father has always been better known than the son. But not so abroad, since the son reached the whole learned world of his day with his discoveries, inventions and theories, he was for many years, as the central figure of the newly founded Académie des Sciences in Paris, one of the most respected scientists of Europe, and later in life, as a kind of elder statesman in the world of science, a figure deeply respected, even by his younger contemporaries Newton and Leibniz. Constantijn was an excellent father who lived to be almost ninety years of age, so that he was able to enjoy the successes and, we believe, also to understand the achievements of his great son.

With Christiaan Huygens we have arrived at the highest point attained by Dutch science of the Golden Century, though we might perhaps be inclined to place van Leeuwenhoek beside him. There is, however, in the Olympian figure of Huygens something that the good and honest municipal employee van Leeuwenhoek could not claim to possess. And this Olympian atmosphere surrounding Huygens during his lifetime has stayed with him, not in the least because of the monumental edition of his collected

works in twenty-two heavy tomes, published with great and loving
care between 1888 and 1950 by the Holland Society of Sciences.
The Dutch may be proud of this edition, all the more since England with its Newton and Germany with its Leibniz have not
been able to achieve a comparable result, though a monumental
edition of Newton's works is at present in the making.

Huygens was born in 1629 in the Hague, studied first in
Leiden, where van Schooten was his teacher, and afterwards at
the Athenaeum in Breda, where John Pell was a teacher, an
Englishman, who has left a name in mathematics.[1] Descartes,
who was a good friend of Constantijn, found a great admirer in
his son. The *Principia Philosophiae* of the great man had been
published in 1644, and Christiaan studied his book with real
passion. "When I read that book", he tells us later, after his position with respect to the Cartesian philosophy had become more
critical, "it seemed to me that everything in the world became
clearer and I was certain that it was due to my ignorance if I met
a difficulty". A correspondence with Marin Mersenne in Paris
aided the young Huygens in finding himself as a mathematician.
His first published work (1651, 1654) dealt with the old problem
of the computation of π, but with new methods, the first essential
progress after Archimedes. Here he also improved on the work of
Grégoire de Saint Vincent. He traveled, and in 1655 he was in
Paris among the scientists in a circle that would soon be part of
the Académie des Sciences. Here he heard that two French savants,
Pascal and Fermat, had been engaged in applying mathematical
considerations to games of chance. After thinking about problems
independently, he put his results on paper under the title of *Van
Rekeningh in Spelen van Geluck* (On the Computation of Games
of Chance), an essay published by van Schooten in 1657 in Latin,
before it appeared in Dutch (1659). Interested in theory as well
as craftsmanship, he engaged in the construction of lenses, clocks,
and telescopes for astronomical purposes. His telescopes were a

great advancement compared to those used by Galileo, and enabled Huygens to discover a moon of Saturn (Titan, 1655) and shortly afterwards the ring of this planet. Following an invitation by Colbert, the powerful advisor of Louis XIV, he moved to Paris in 1666 to become a member of the Académie des Sciences founded the same year. He stayed in Paris as an honored academician till 1675. Here he published his great work on pendulum clocks, the *Horologium oscillatorium*, also a great step ahead in the new mechanics and the new mathematics (1673). He spent his later years on the family estate 'Hofwijck', near the Hague, where he developed in the *Traité de la lumière* (1690) his new theory of light founded on the transmission of waves. He died in 1695. His *Kosmotheoros*, a book with suggestions on life on other planets, appeared in 1698. 'Hofwijck' is now a museum.

It strikes us as a curious thing that Huygens quietly continued his activities at the Académie in Paris in 1672 at a time when Louis XIV violated his country; and he even dedicated his book on pendulum clocks to Louis. This was the year in which both England and France and two German bishops invaded the Republic, at first with such alarming success that a wild panic broke out, in which the brothers De Witt were assassinated. The young stadhouder William III, placed in charge of the defense, was able to check the invasion and save the Republic. Huygens was far from indifferent to the fate of his native country, but there was a cosmopolitanism in that seventeenth century world of scientists and scholars that was hardly at all disturbed even by such kind of warfare. It was also in 1672 that Swammerdam made an appeal to the Royal Society in enemy London concerning a scientific dispute with Dutch colleagues. The wars that raged almost without cessation here, there and everywhere were, in most cases, commercial wars parading as dynastic conflicts carried on in an impersonal and "scientific" way with mercenary soldiers and professional officers, so that we can follow the whole development

of science and philosophy of that period, the continuous growth
of the mechanical picture of the world, without paying more than
superficial attention to the wars of the days. This is typical for the
high days of mercantilism and begins to change somewhat with
the industrial revolution and the Napoleonic wars, though the scientific ideal that embraces international collaboration was never
entirely abandoned even in the period of the worst hatred and
murder of the twentieth century. It has remained alive, despite
cold and hot wars, and we can only hope for the best for the
future.

Huygens' work shows also the characteristics common to the
work of almost all leading seventeenth-century mathematicians
and philosophers; a deep understanding of the relation between
theory and practice, a keen power of observation, mastery of
mathematical technique and the technique of instrumentation,
as well as a profound feeling for the essential. We can see it in
his theory of chance, in his astronomical computations and discoveries — which added new power of conviction to the theory
of Copernicus — in his introduction of pendulum clocks, his
theory of light and his contributions to what was soon to be
known as the differential and integral calculus. We can also think
of his pioneering work in mechanics: the theory of collision and
his introduction of centripetal forces. He even experimented for
a while on static electricity following some experiments published
by the Magdeburg burgomaster Otto (von) Gericke. These were
all special contributions, each of them enough to remember his
name as a scientist, but nevertheless all related to each other.
Huygens knew this himself, and now, looking back to the science
of the mercantilist period, we see it all more clearly in its historical
setting.

This was the time in which strong bureaucratic states were formed, more and more depending on regular taxation, states against
which the Republic of the Seven Provinces with its federative

system could not hold its own in the long run, although during the Golden Century there was at least a kind of parity. Here were states under whose protection merchants were engaged in commerce and bankers in finance, and since industry was still on a comparatively smaller scale the philosophy of the state was directed primarily to promote this commerce. "There is more to be earned by manufacture than by agriculture, and more by commerce than by industry", wrote William Petty and praised Holland as an example of how a country could be rich through commerce. But to become rich through commerce meant a favorable "balance of trade" and such a favorable balance of trade was obtained in the first place by overseas enterprises, which imported raw materials and exported manufactured products. Mercantilists, such as Colbert, therefore encouraged manufacture in their country, above all to reach a favorable balance of trade and thus obtain gold in their treasury. This is the principal reason that so much attention in that time was paid to navigation. The states themselves through academies, scientific expedition, premiums or honorary titles encouraged the scientists to pay attention to those sciences that were useful to navigation, astronomy, mechanics, optics and cartography. Interest also centered on such sciences as botany and mineralogy, mainly for utilitarian reasons. These motives were not the only reason for the encouragement of the natural sciences, since the search for knowledge of nature and even straight curiosity played a role, but in all government actions of that time great importance was placed on the balance of trade and its requirements.

This encouragement on the part of the authorities contributed to the great success of the new method, the application of mathematics to mechanics and mechanics to the whole known picture of the world, and to the cultivation of experiments. As we said, scientific curiosity, the passion for knowledge, was stimulated to a high degree. Every experiment could lead to something new, to something great, not only for the purpose of economic advantage, but also of new insight. The *burgher* class, especially that rich and powerful minority that in all mercantilist countries was engaged in a kind of alliance with the reigning monarchy and remaining feudal elements, except in Holland where such an alliance was not necessary, felt confident in its conviction that control over nature was possible, just as overseas it had obtained control over large sections of the Asian and American world. In its most philosophically interested circles that followed the leadership of a Descartes or Bacon and who, towards the end of the century, would recognize in Newton a new and even greater leader, this *haute bourgeoisie* encouraged this search for an outlook on the world that could explain the whole of nature and lead to new discoveries and inventions in an unlimited way. If we try to understand Huygens' importance in the framework of this general program, we easily find two leading thoughts present in much of his work, a practical and a theoretical one in intimate relationship. On the practical side he looks for a solution to the age-old problem of the determination of the geographic longitude at sea. Wherever we look in sixteenth- and seventeenth-century natural science, we can rarely escape this problem. For navigation it was especially vital. The larger and more expensive the ships, and the more successful the progress of science, the more the difficulty in determining this longitude was felt as a humiliation to the human mind. The existing clocks and astronomic tables could not prevent shipwrecks: even in the eighteenth century huge ships were wrecked near the coasts as a result of faulty determination of longitude, particularly by night and in bad weather. Some people began to consider the problem as something like the quadrature of the circle, hunting for the perpetuum mobile, or looking for the philosophical stone. The problem was popular enough to move literary pens: Jonathan Swift, creator of Gulliver, even dedicated an ode to this subject. Modesty prevents us from quoting it.

Huygens' contribution has above all been the invention of the pendulum clocks. For years he devoted long hours to experiments with them, constructing instruments that measured time better than existing clocks, but was disappointed in finding that they were not as successful at sea as he had hoped. The rolling and pitching of the majestic frigates was a very disturbing factor, apart from the fact that the length of the pendulum with a one second period is dependent on its position on earth. On land these difficulties did not arise and pendulum clocks readily found their use in astronomical work. Huygens also experimented with spiral springs, but the problem of the exact determination of longitude at sea remained unsolved for almost another century.

Science has greatly profited from this search for a solution of the irritating problem and not only through the efforts of Huygens alone. The necessity of solving it was one of the principal reasons for the foundation of the Greenwich astronomical observatory in 1676, during the early years of the Royal Society, the English Academy of Sciences. We already mentioned how Cassini and Roemer in Paris were inspired in their work by this longitude problem. When Robert Hooke, the great mechanic and microscopist of the Royal Society, experimented with spiral springs for the improvement of clocks, he discovered the principal law of the theory of elasticity named after him. And Newton, in his famous work, the *Principia* of 1687, which deals in many places with theoretical questions related to navigation, laid the first foundation of a good lunar theory.

This lunar theory as an application of the so-called three body problem [2] at last produced the "celestial clock" in which longitude at sea could actually be found by computation. This was in the middle of the eighteenth century; with it the names of Leonhard Euler and Tobias Mayer are connected. Around the same time England and French instrument makers constructed clocks called chronometers with such a measure of accuracy that the solution of the age-old problem with the aid of terrestrial clocks was made possible. Connected with this are the names of "Chronometer" John Harrison in England and Jean-Baptiste Le Roy in France. These methods came only into general use during the nineteenth century. At present we do not only have chronometers but also radio signals and, of course, also excellent maps.

2

In his theoretical considerations Huygens espoused a consistent materialism which, following Descartes, formed the "true philosophy", in which the causes of all natural actions are reduced to mechanical causes". This was Huygens' own formulation in his theory of light. He saw this mechanical explanation in the impact of small particles obeying mathematically determined mechanical laws. The theory of atoms, already developed in antiquity, but overshadowed by the authority of Aristotle and Plato, gained a new respect with the new science. The moving mass particles whose behavior could so nicely be expressed by mathematical formulas and expressed in such an acceptable way by an abstract causality principle, became more and more the elements in the explanation of nature. Some people have seen in these abstract, causally-connected individual atoms a reflection of the *burgher* society in which the personal ties between the individuals have been replaced by abstract social laws in the market place. Such an explanation tends to forget that modern science considered not only atoms in its discussion of matter, but also the continuous and infinitely divisible field, at present as well as in the time of Descartes. It is true that *burgher* society stimulated greatly the causal, mathematically founded, mechanical discussion of matter, but the special theories usually found their reason of existence

in the objective reality of nature as well as in many other factors
– traditions, etc. – apart from direct social relationships.

Huygens' relation to Descartes is somewhat comparable to
Kepler's relation to Copernicus, the man who carries out a program and corrects it at the same time. Where Descartes only ascribed extension to matter, Huygens gave it solidity and recognized
the existence of larger and smaller elementary particles. The metaphysical, dogmatic, element in Descartes was alien to Huygens;
in his gradual emancipation from his youthful ideal he saw the
natural phenomena in a more concrete way and was deeply involved
in the experimental side of the new science. This experimental side
of his work is related to his theory, which here becomes a real
dynamics. We see it in his theory of collision, in his theory of
the pendulum and in his theory of light. In his mechanics he
introduced a principle that we now recognize as a law of conservation of energy. He also computed the force which keeps a moving
mass point in uniform circular motion; this was great progress in
the development of the principle of inertia as we have witnessed
it in imperfect form with Beeckman. Light in Huygens' theory
has its origin in vibrations of the elastic particles of an extremely
rarified medium called ether, analogous to sound which is produced
by vibrations of particles of the air. But this theory of light also
shows Huygens' inclination to experiment. because he investigated the so-called double refraction that appears when light
passes through transparent calcareous spar crystals, known as
Iceland spar. This wave theory of light had to wait long for its
acceptance because of the authority of Newton, whose very influential *Opticks* of 1704 taught that light exists of moving particles. In the nineteenth century Huygens' theory was confirmed
by newer investigations, and now the term light waves as well
as radio waves is in general use, the term light quanta reminding
us of Newton's particles.

Huygens' mechanical materialism was based on the theory that

the elementary particles of matter could only influence each other
by direct contact. When, in 1687, Newton, in his *Principia*, based
his mechanics on the action at distance between particles which
attract each other through empty space with a force with the
Aristotelian name of "gravity", Huygens found it difficult to
accept this theory. It seemed to him that Newton's opinion was
a step backward compared to the principles developed by Galileo,
Descartes and himself. Leibniz, Newton's contemporary, shared
this feeling of displeasure, which he also extended to Newton's
theory of an absolute and empty space in which bodies move in
an absolute uniformly moving time, both space and time independent of matter. Huygens also had trouble in understanding those
fluxions and infinitesimals used by Newton and Leibniz in their
foundation of the new differential and integral calculus, which
have a metaphysical touch absent in the ancient "exhaustion"
methods as used by Archimedes. But Newton accomplished something which neither Huygens nor Leibniz could achieve: the construction of a great mathematical system of the world based in
the same way on axioms as Euclid had achieved it in geometry.
It was possible to build for centuries on the foundation Newton
had laid, and only in the present century has it been possible to
revise Newton's ideas in such a way as to take Huygens' and
Leibniz's objections into account, though the relation of mass to
gravity, of matter to space and time remains one of the great
problems of physics.

3

Although with the Cartesians, who after about 1650 became more
and more prominent in the world of mathematicians, physicists,
physicians and philosophers, we have passed generally speaking
from the "common man" to the patricians and their protégés,

we must not think that the stalwart schoolmasters, surveyors
and engineers of the first half of the Golden Century later disappeared. However, compared with men as Cartesius, De Witt,
Hudde, van Schooten and Huygens men like Gietermaker or
Kinckhuysen, in their way clever teachers of mathematics, take
only a back seat. We should not think either that all leading
Cartesians either belonged to the patrician class or were directly
related to it through a university position or relations with such
persons as Elizabeth of the Palatinate. An example is Spinoza, also
a product of the Cartesian school who, though related to the
merchant class, retired into a modest way of life, where he se-
lected the profession of a lens grinder, a profession modest, but
modern for his time. Yet, in a larger sense he remains representative of the Cartesianizing Regent class. He achieved his intellectual position by bringing the political and philosophical ideas
of the most conscious leaders of the Regent caste to such radical
perfection, that only very few of them were willing to be seen
with him in public. Already, at that time in its triumphant rise
to power, the *haute bourgeoisie* and its followers were somewhat
afraid of the consequences of their own principles.

Spinoza's more open friends were not to be found among members of the Reformed Church, for even the most latitudinarian
of them were not willing to trespass on the premises of the Regent
establishment. Spinoza found his friends among those intellectuals
that neither belonged to the ruling class nor to traditional protestantism, the Rijnsburg collegians, a sect reminiscent of the
Quakers.[3] But Spinoza was also in contact with the leaders of the
new natural science inspired by Bacon and Descartes, cultivated in
England, France, Germany and Sweden under princely protection.
We only mention his personal contact with Henry Oldenburg,
secretary of the newly founded Royal Society in London. Young
Leibniz also came to pay his respects, not without a certain amount
of trepidation. We know that Hudde, Huygens, De Witt and other

learned patricians had great respect for Spinoza, but they were too much men of the world to compromise their class position *sub specie eternitatis.*

We should not think of Spinoza, the grinder of lenses, as an old-fashioned craftsman, a colleague of the baker, the butcher and the candlestick maker. In Spinoza's time the grinding of lenses was as up-to-date as the making of electronic apparatus is at present. In those days of budding telescopy and microscopy and of new research into the nature of light, lenses were the great tools for experimental investigation. Huygens and van Leeuwenhoek were grinders of lenses, Nicolaas Hartsoeker was so famous that Czar Peter wanted to bring him to Russia. Famous was also Samuel van Musschenbroek, and burgomaster Hudde was deeply interested.[4] Spinoza's treatise on the rainbow, a typical Cartesian subject, is also connected with his optical work. This treatise was only published in 1687, after Spinoza's death, as *Stelkonstige Reeckening van den Regenboog.* It is also believed that a short *Reeckening van Kanssen* (Theory of chances) came out of Spinoza's pen.

The question may be asked why Holland, so far advanced in mathematics and mechanics and on whose territory Cartesius and Spinoza developed great mathematically based philosophical systems, never produced the great mathematical synthesis connected with the name of Newton. Some people will deny the right to ask such a question: genius has nothing to do with nationality, the laws concerning the origin of genius belong to the domain of the accidental. We shall not here go into this question, only observe that it is not entirely accidental that the decisive work after all came from England. In England we have the Royal Society and thus the possibility of constant contact between clever minds. In Holland, most people worked for themselves only or at most, with a few other persons. Descartes was a Frenchman, Spinoza a Jew largely avoided, Huygens spent many years in France. There was little organizational initiative in the domain of science. Already in the nineteenth century Busken Huet made a similar observation: "There was no naval training school, no military academy, not one agricultural, not one industrial, not one commercial school. Why should there have been an academy of arts?" And why an Academy of Sciences? Some attempts, made in 1664, to organize a circle in Amsterdam for the study of comparative anatomy never got far underway. There was too little centralization for this kind of activity. Every province, every town was a little world unto itself. There was little room for teamwork. But it may be possible to write an interesting history of science for many a special town — such as Hoorn, Enkhuizen, Middelburg, Franeker, Dordrecht, Amsterdam — a history that may contain much that is little known and very interesting.

CHAPTER IX

THE LIVING WORLD

1

At the time of Jan De Witt there were already five universities. The oldest was that of Leiden, founded in 1575 after the triumph over the Spanish. This was in Holland. Then followed those of Franeker in Frisia in 1585, of Harderwijk in Gelderland in 1603, of Groningen in the province of Groningen in 1614 and of Utrecht in the province of Utrecht in 1636. In addition there were Latin schools and Athenaea, as those of Dordrecht, Breda and Deventer. The most famous Athenaeum was in Amsterdam and its status almost equalled that of a university. It dated from 1632 and is the forerunner of the present university. The astronomical observatory at Leiden was founded in 1633, that of Utrecht in 1642.[1] Lectures were given, and textbooks written, in Latin.

The universities were primarily schools for the training of Reformed ministers, but they did not neglect the secular sciences, and from the beginning leading figures are found in the chairs. This was a much better situation than existed at many a university in other countries. Yet, it remained a fact that the really great ideas of the natural sciences and philosophy were generated in the world outside the schools – think of Stevin, Descartes, Swammerdam and van Leeuwenhoek; just as in modern times we find a similar situation in the economic sciences – think of Adam Smith, Ricardo, Marx. But though the names of the seventeenth-century scientists and philosophers we just mentioned are well known to this day, if we ask ourselves how many of the *academic* worthies of those days are still widely remembered, the harvest is pretty meager.

First to mind perhaps comes Snellius, since his name can be found in most textbooks on physics in conjunction with his law of refraction. But, to give an English version of an old Dutch verse, "contemporaries oft bestow their praise or blame quite differently from the merits grandsons claim", and this holds not only for poets and painters, but also for learned ladies and gentlemen. In their day professors such as Golius, Burgersdicius, van Schooten, Hortensius, Metius, Blasius, Vossius and others were known far and wide; so was Franco Burgersdicius' Aristotelian-Ramist logic for a while a highly esteemed text in Cambridge and even at Harvard College in New England. Among the excellent physicians of the Republic in the seventeenth century Nicolaas Tulp may well be the best known, if only as the central figure of Rembrandt's "Anatomical Lesson" (1632).[2] As the principal author of a *Pharmacopeia* (1636), the first in the Netherlands, and a number of medical observations, highly valued until deep in the eighteenth century, he is almost forgotten, except in professional circles; in 1936 a medal was issued in commemoration of this *Pharmacopeia*. Other medical names we see occasionally mentioned outside of medical history are those of Frederick Ruysch, the father of the flower paintress Rachel Ruysch, and Reinier de Graaf, the discoverer of the "Grafian follicles" in the ovaries. Let us pause for a moment for a look at these once so famous men.

Van Schooten and Metius we have already met. Jacobus Golius (van Gool) was the successor of Snellius as professor of mathematics at Leiden and the founder of the astronomical observatory in 1633. He was also a distinguished orientalist, editor of Arabic texts, among them the astronomical treatise of Al-Farghāni (ninth century), published posthumously in 1667 with a Latin translation and commentary.

Franciscus Burgersdicius (Burgersdijk) was professor of

philosophy at Leiden from 1628 until his death in 1635. Of his logic (1626) at least twenty-nine editions are known.[3]

Martinus Hortensius (van den Hove) was a collaborator of van Lansberge in Middelburg. From 1634 to his early death in 1639 he taught mathematics at the Amsterdam Athenaeum and was, with van Lansberge, an early promoter of the Copernican system. In 1635 he was appointed with Blaeu and some others to the committee that was to invite Galileo to come to Holland, especially in connection with his method of finding longitude at sea, and to offer him a golden chain. Nothing came of it; Galileo, already in trouble with the Inquisition, had no desire to get more involved with Dutch heretics, if he could help it.

Gerardus Blasius (Blaes), a native of Flanders, studied medicine in Copenhagen and Leiden, became a physician in Amsterdam and, in 1660, the first professor of medicine at the Athenaeum. He collaborated with Swammerdam and De Graaf (with whom he had a priority dispute) on the anatomy and the physiology of man and the animals. We shall meet these men again when we discuss the teaching of Sylvius.

Gerardus Joannes Vossius and his son Isaac were extremely erudite, and outstanding Latinists. The father was professor in Leiden from 1620 to 1631 and from then till his death in 1649, professor at the Amsterdam Athenaeum; the son was librarian of Christina of Sweden and afterwards lived in London from 1670 until his death in 1689. His enormous collection of manuscripts became the *codex Vossianus* of the university library of Leiden. The father wrote a history of mathematics as part of a whole group of similar summaries in astronomy, cartography, philosophy, etc., and the son was the author of some works of a physical geographical character, where he showed himself as one of the first scientific students of ocean currents and winds. They are still remembered in Amsterdam in the name of the Vossius lyceum — where I once had the pleasure to be a teacher.

2

There were already good physicians in the Northern Netherlands during the Spanish period, although Volcker Koyter from Groningen had to travel abroad to make his name as an embryologist and anatomist. Others returned after a stay abroad, as Johannes Wier (Weyer), back in the Netherlands at the age of twenty-five, and from 1555 onwards, for many years, personal physician to the humanistically inclined Count William of Gulik and Cleve. This physician, we saw, was one of the first to take a critical stand on the reigning craze of witchhunting; in a (Latin) book of 1577 he asked for medical examination rather than torture in the case of persons accused of witchcraft. Few at that time listened to him.

His contemporary Pieter van Foreest, of an ancient Dutch patrician family, settled, after a stay abroad, in 1546 at the age of twenty-four, in his native Alkmaar. Here, and after 1558 in Delft, where he died in 1597, he remained as a hard-working and honored municipal physician. He deserves admiration as a pioneer in a field that even at present lacks the interest it deserves, namely preventive medicine. The task of the physician still remains primarily the curing of an illness after it has occurred, whereas the task of preventing misfortune remains number two on the program; every slum, every polluted place can bear witness to it. Doctor van Foreest advocated improved water supplies, refreshing of the city canals, better hygiene. He was a good observer in the Renaissance spirit of Vesalius, and his textbook of clinical medicine with sections on surgery and gynecology was for many years a standard work. He also was physician to William the Silent and performed the post mortem after the assassination.

One of the reasons that medical research could flourish in the Republic was the relative ease with which physicians could obtain corpses for their anatomical and pathological research and instruction. Clerical prejudice against dissection of human bodies was not

as strong in the Republic as in some other countries. It was not
so very difficult to obtain bodies of executed persons, but these
were usually bodies of healthy people and could not be used for
research into pathological cases. But the possibility of studying
pathological cases did exist and all this study of bodies was of
great benefit to the medical profession; Dutch anatomists of the
seventeenth century added greatly to our knowledge of anatomy
of man and animal. Anatomical lessons were often given in public
and received considerable attention; we know of a case in Dordrecht
dealing with the body of a woman who had died of kidney stones,
her case studied in *praesentia plurimarum matronarum* – in the
presence of many matrons. The book of Vesalius opens with a
beautiful picture of an anatomical lesson and Dutch artists sub-
sequently, more than once, immortalized such lessons.

Let us return to Tulp, the Amsterdam lecturer on anatomy. He
had studied in Leiden, was for more than half a century a popular
medical practitioner in Amsterdam and also a prominent member
of the Regent class, syndic, member of the board of the orphan
asylum, curator of the Athenaeum and four times burgomaster.
It is said that he was the first to visit his patients in a horse-drawn
carriage.[4] Among his books there is one in Latin dealing with a
number of cases of disease that passed through many reprints after
its first appearance in 1641 and was translated into Dutch. He
is also considered the first to describe an orangutan – or so he
thought – but the animal came from Africa and thus must have
been either a gorilla or chimpanzee.[5] Tulp died in 1674 at the age
of eighty-one in the Hague.

3

In the sixteenth and seventeenth centuries we find physicians
engaged in various sciences different from medicine. At many

universities the medical faculty was the only place where lectures were held on the natural sciences, so that men interested in mathematics, physics, or natural history first had to complete their medical studies. We have already met Gemma Frisius and Jacob van Deventer, medical men who were cartographers. At the time of van Linschoten we find in Enkhuizen the municipal doctor Bernardus Paludanus (Van den Broecke) who on his travels had gathered a great number of plants, animals and minerals, and kept his collection open to the public. We find him also in Linschoten's *Itenerario* with an article on plants from India. Many botanists or zoologists of those days had, like Paludanus, studied medicine. Dodoens and L'Obell are other examples. Clusius and Snellius, however, had studied law.

Descartes had also studied medicine and his philosophy was very attractive to representatives of the medical profession. Among his pupils we find Henri le Roy or Regius, first rector of the Latin School in Naarden and in 1639 professor of medicine at the then new university of Utrecht. In 1646 he defended Harvey's theory of the circulation of the blood and came out openly for the Copernican theory, thus venturing beyond his master. But his differences with Descartes became more marked when he published his *Fundamenta physices* (1646). In this book, dedicated to Prince Frederick Henry, he tried to conquer Cartesian dualism by pointing out the intimate relationship between soul and body. The soul, taught Regius, is dependent on the body: "If the head receives a serious blow, then thinking stops. If the head is cured, thinking returns soon afterwards." Medical men who more than anybody else could observe the influence of bodily functions on our state of mind, have often been inclined towards materialism, if only a mechanical materialism; as is sometimes said: *tres medici, duo athei*. We know that Descartes was deeply offended by Regius' amendments and Regius has sometimes been called an apostate. But Descartes' protests did not invalidate Regius' reasoning and we find his ideas again in the writings of the French materialists of the next century. Regius had to face quite a lot of opposition during his lifetime, although officially he adhered to the tenets of the Dordrecht Synod. But the Voetians did not care for him because of his belief in the Copernican theory, his materialism and his disbelief in the portentous properties of the comets, so that they considered him an even greater enemy than Descartes. But he survived all opposition, survived even the formidable Voetius and died in 1671 at the age of eighty-one. He deserves more attention from the students of materialism than he has received so far.

Another pupil of the Cartesian school with medical training was François dele Boë or Franciscus Sylvius (Dele Boë being Languedoc for Du Bois) from Hanau in Germany, student at Leiden, Wittenberg and other universities and from 1638 until his death in 1672, connected with the University of Leiden, from 1658 on as a professor of medicine.[6] Where Descartes stressed the mechanical action of the body, Sylvius stressed the chemical aspect. We are used to characterizing the Cartesian approach as iatrophysics, the Sylvian as iatrochemistry. This iatrochemistry, as already noted, went back to Paracelsus and van Helmont and found its most brilliant supporter in Sylvius. He studied the chemical actions of metabolism, stressing the affinity of salts and alkaloids, and as a good pupil of van Helmont investigated fermentation as a cause of physiological and pathological processes and hence of all vital action. In therapeutics he preferred the new chemical drugs such as mercury and antimony to the ancient Galenic ones and also opposed Galen as one of the first defenders of Harvey's theory of the circulation of the blood. He used dogs in his experimentation.[7]

Like his older colleague van Schooten, Sylvius seems to have been a good and inspiring teacher: we get the impression of a vivid intellectual life in his Leiden circle during the 1660s and 1670s with such pupils as Swammerdam, De Graaf, Ruysch and the Dane Stensen, all famous in their day, and later colleagues such as Johannes van Horne (Hornius), from 1653 to 1670 professor of anatomy and surgery. In this circle methods were developed to conserve anatomical preparations by means of a clever injection of certain liquids into body vessels, thus solving the ancient problem of preserving organs taken from dead bodies against corruption. Sylvius was one of the first to take students with him to the hospital for individual clinical instruction, a practice introduced by his predecessor Heurnius. It is said that he could find much good and little evil in smoking a pipe, if the puffing of this controversial weed was not overdone.[8]

In 1664 Reinier de Graaf, one of Sylvius' most illustrious pupils, completed under him his essay on the pancreas, and after staying a while in France where he got his medical degree in 1668, became a physician in Delft where he made the acquaintance of van Leeuwenhoek. He was one of the first to do fundamental anatomical research of the generative organs of men and mammals; for his two books on this subject, published in 1668 and 1672, he drew the many illustrations himself. We have already mentioned the follicles named after him. He believed he had found the eggs in the ovary, an error only corrected much later. De Graaf died young, not older than thirty-two years of age; an unhappy conflict with his fellow student Swammerdam in connection with the discovery of these follicles poisoned the last year of his life. His name has remained alive in the medical world through his collected works, republished and translated more than once. He is sometimes considered one of the founders of experimental physiology.

With de Graaf's fellow student Frederick Ruysch we come to a physician with merits both as a botanist and as a maker of medical preparations. He obtained his doctor's degree in 1664 under Sylvius, practiced first in the Hague, then in Amsterdam and, in 1685, when the botanical garden (hortus) in the Plantage was finished, he became professor of botany at the Athenaeum. Where de Graaf only reached his thirty-second year, Ruysch made it to the age of ninety-three. Till his death in 1731 he was a zealous collector, known for the clever way in which he knew how to prepare his anatomical and pathological specimens. Where formerly attempts at preservation were made by filling arteries and other vessels with air, the new technique of conservation used by Ruysch was based on injecting into the organs other materials such as wax. These techniques, we saw, seem to have been developed in the school of Sylvius, because Swammerdam also used them and has even been mentioned as the inventor. Ruysch's museum was sold in 1717 to Czar Peter of Russia for 30,000 guilders, and the story goes that the collection arrived in deplorable condition because the stalwart tars could not keep away from the alcohol of the preparations. The story is a good one, but, as so many good stories, it limps, since the collection still exists in Leningrad among the treasures of the Academy of Sciences. A catalogue of 1947 mentioned nine hundred and thirty-five preparations.[9] After the sale Ruysch continued to collect with undiminished zeal. His new collection was sold, after his death, for 20,000 guilders to Peter's competitor, the King of Poland. Ruysch wrote many books which were beautifully illustrated by himself and his daughter. The old gentleman loved to display the skeletons in his collection in all kinds of interesting positions complete with edifying mottos.

A physician and contemporary of Ruysch who also lived till deep into the eighteenth century was Hendrik van Deventer. He became known as an obstetrician with the already mentioned Labadists when they established themselves after 1675 at their Frisian castle. He began as an apprentice to a goldsmith and had already made a great name for himself before he was examined in medicine in Groningen. He remained, however, without full official qualification. It seems that it did not harm him in his practice, carried on in Voorburg near the Hague after the sect was dissolved. His books, based on his large practice and written in Dutch, were very popular in his day and were used by physicians and midwives alike for help in simple as well as difficult deliveries. The title of one of these books is *Dageraet der Vroetvrouwen* (Dawn of the Midwives). He died in 1724.

3

The medieval monasteries already had their herb gardens, and even if the monasteries disappeared, the knowledge of the medicinal virtue of plants was not lost. For a long time this aspect of botany as well as the study of agricultural plants was almost the sole field of interest. Botanical books described mostly useful plants, botanists usually restricted themselves to collecting and a rather superficial form of classification. Change came in the sixteenth century when some outstanding humanist scientists began to take up the study of botany for its own sake. We think, for instance, of the German Leonhart Fuchs after whom the fuchsia is named, of Dodoens and of Clusius. The *Hortus Botanicus*, the botanical garden at Leiden, goes back to the early years of the university; and in these early years there were already two distinguished botanists appointed as professors. Founded in 1587, it was only really started in 1594 with the arrival of Carolus Clusius, who, from 1593 till his death in 1609, taught botany in Leiden. Clusius was preceded at Leiden by Rembert Dodoens (Rembertus Dodonaeus), one of the great collectors of his age. His *Cruydtboeck* (Herbal) appeared for the first time in 1554, was repeatedly enlarged, reprinted and translated and has already the beginning of a systematic classification. He died in 1585 after only a few years at Leiden.

Clusius (Charles de l'Ecluse) was director of the botanical garden of the emperor at Vienna before he came to Leiden. He was particularly interested in plants from all over the world, collecting them personally on his travels in Europe and Asia or through contact and correspondence with colleagues and friends, so that the Hortus in Leiden could already display about one thousand different plants at the beginning of the seventeenth century.[10] Clusius played an important role in the introduction of the famous Dutch culture of flower bulbs, and especially the introduction of the tulip, a native of Southern Europe and Asia Minor.[11] These bulbs were, for a while, the subject of speculation, a favorite occupation of many a Dutch capitalist, ending up in a mania known as the foolish tulip trade of 1636–1637, years in which fantastic prices were paid for the bulbs. This speculation eventually led to a collapse of the market, the ruination of many a speculator and the continuation of the trade on a more reasonable scale. In his novel *La tulipe noire*, Dumas sketched how much the well-to-do Dutchman continued to admire his tulips, especially the rare variations.

Later in the century other botanical gardens were founded in Utrecht, Groningen and Amsterdam; with the Amsterdam *Hortus* the names of Dr. Ruysch and the Commelin family are connected. Linnaeus named a genus of plants after these brothers, a genus related to the spider wort (tradescantia).[12] Rich collectors were also after minerals, objects of art and curios; ships from America and Asia brought in a large variety of such articles. Schools and patrician houses had cabinets with shells, stuffed animals, skeletons of man and beast, artifacts, precious books, maps, etc. We see them on pictures of that period: deer heads stick out of the walls, globes and huge volumes invite study or perhaps only the envy of neighbors. We know of no less than a thousand of those private museums in the Republic. The physicians had medical collections, like that of Dr. Ruysch boasting of preparations and sometimes of beautifully adorned moralizing skeletons. A well-known *rariteiten-kabinet* was that of the Amsterdam apothecary Jan Jacobsz. Swammerdam, a generation before Ruysch (he died in 1678), containing old porcelain, medals, corals and shells, but also boasting of "a little Chinese image made of silver, a little golden Japanese idol, the face of Gustavus Adolphus in gold relief, an artificial mouse with copper wheels and iron springs", for which he wanted 60,000 guilders (but did not get). This all looks very attractive, but rather superficial. In general, we can say that during the Golden Century more attention was paid to the increase in depth of the mathematical and mechanical sciences than that of biology. For a long time biology was mainly occupied with collecting and a rather superficial method of classi- fication. This is true particularly for the period before 1660 and was an international phenomenon. Neither Bacon nor Descartes were very much interested in a more scientific biology, although the deepening of natural history occurs also in their school. The deeper study of biology was only thoroughly undertaken after the solution of the burning questions in navigation, astronomy, mechanics, optics and mathematics had progressed to a consider- able extent. Is it accidental that the representatives of the Dutch aristocracy who made a name in science, Hudde, De Witt, Huygens, also made that name in mathematics and mechanics, while the new discoveries in biology are connected with the names of Swammerdam and van Leeuwenhoek, both certainly not of patri- cian stock? The mercantilist period knew two scientific dictators: Newton, the oracle of the physical, Linnaeus that of the biological world, but Linnaeus came half a century after Newton.

The great discoveries in biology and medicine were closely related to the new inventions in optics. We have seen how lenses were appreciated, how the telescope helped to enlarge the picture of the world. Now the microscope began to take its place next to the telescope. Galileo, the first to use the telescope for scientific purposes, may well have been the first or one of the first to do some research with the microscope. But the great triumphs of microscopy date from the later years of the seventeenth century. Several scientists in Holland worked with the microscope, or rather with the magnifying glass, because composite microscopes were still a rarity. Ruysch and De Graaf used the magnifying glass in their medical work and Swammerdam in the investigation of insects. But the greatest Dutch microscopist, whose name is still mentioned together with that of Swammerdam, and who is respected all over the world, was Anthoni van Leeuwenhoek. These four men were more or less contemporaries, born between 1632 and 1641, but two of them died young. Ruysch and van Leeuwenhoek lived to a ripe age.

4

Jan Swammerdam was the son of Jan Jacobsz. Swammerdam, the collector of curiosities. We have met the son already in Leiden as a pupil of Professor Sylvius and mentioned his friendship with De Graaf and Steno. For a while he was with Steno in Paris where he frequented those scientific circles, which were soon to form the Académie des Sciences. Here we also met Huygens. Steno (Stensen) later became wellknown in Florence and Copenhagen as a geologist and anatomist; the 'ductus stenoni' (stenonianus)[13] connecting nose and mouth cavities was named for him. Swammerdam returned to Holland, received his medical degree in 1667 with his thesis on breathing, but did not become a medical practitioner. He had another vocation, the study of 'small animals', especially 'bloodless animals', namely insects. He gave all his energy and time to his lifework, spent on it the money that his father gave him, not too willingly, and worked with such zeal on his objects and preparations that his health was severely damaged. Eventually he fell into a mystical melancholy state and died in 1680, only forty-three years old: a man who indeed worked himself to death for science. Nobody ever studied with more love bees, mayflies, wasps and other insects

he investigated air, water, earth, land, field, meadow, pasture, wasteland, dune, riverside, beach, river, stagnant water, lakes, sea, pit, herb, ruin, holes, residential places, yes, even privies: so that he could find the little eggs, little worms, little pupas, the little butterflies; and might learn their nests, nourishment, mode of living, melodies, changings and groupings,

writes Boerhaave. And in this way Swammerdam investigated everything concerning insects, their anatomical composition, their development and mode of living. This mode of living we now call ecology, but Swammerdam sometimes loved a moralizing ecology: "An image of the life of man, shown in the marvels and unheard history of the flying and one-day living mayfly" (1675). He dissected the little animals and studied their members and insides with his magnifying glass, described what he saw with exactitude and added the drawings. He preserved his preparations with a new method that he published in 1672; we have seen that Ruysch, his friend from college, also used this method which was developed in the school of Sylvius. "He often spent a whole day in cleaning the fats in this manner off the body of a single caterpillar in order to find the true construction of the insect's heart." Again we follow Boerhaave. In his *Algemeene verhandeling van de bloedeloose dierkens* (General treatment of bloodless animals) (1669) Swammerdam laid the foundation for a natural classification of insects. Here his primary attention was focused on the different ways of development, a method never used before.

Swammerdam, in contrast to the more rationalizing Cartesians, stressed above all the experiment. He belonged to the school for which one fact has more value than all theories and of which we begin to hear more and more towards the end of the seventeenth century with its developing chemistry and biology. During his life not many of his writings were published and many of his manuscripts have been lost. What remained was only published by Boerhaave in 1737–1738, in three heavy volumes under the name *Bible of Nature* (Biblia Naturae) with a stately Latin translation

next to the homespun Dutch text. Here we find what Swammerdam
wrote on invertebrates and vertebrates and in particular the great
essay on bees. In this essay, the product of years of anatomical
and ecological study, we find for the first time an almost complete
description of what happens in a beehive and about which there
was so much misunderstanding going back to Aristotle: "I would
therefore here right in the beginning inform the reader that
throughout this whole treatise I shall call the pretended king by
the name of the female bee and to that which is commonly called
the drone, I shall give the title of the male bee, while the common
bees I shall for distinction's sake denominate working bee; I shall
also in the following pages show the very clear and evident reasons
which have induced me to make this innovation".

He therefore discovered the existence of the female and also
the nature of the working bees as "sexless females", "as natural
eunuchs [van ontijdigh geslacht] so to speak though in their structure they approach nearer to the female than the male sex". Also
the anatomy of larva, nymph and various adult forms are found
in all details together with excellent drawings. But much more
can be found in Swammerdam than bees or insects alone. For the
knowledge of propagation his studies of the sexual organs of the
frog and his experiments on fertilization are of great interest. It
is a pity that the *Bible of Nature* is an old and expensive book;
parts of it could be reprinted very well in a modern edition. There
exists a small German anthology.

5

Swammerdam, pioneer in the study of entomology with the magnifying glass, looked at things of which the existence was known:
mouths of bees and hearts of caterpillars. Van Leeuwenhoek
passed far beyond this and with his microscopes became the

discoverer of a new world, hardly even suspected. This modest resident of Delft first kept a linendraper's shop in Amsterdam, which he continued for a while in Delft; later he became a Chamberlain of the Lord's Sheriffs [Schepenen] of his native city, also wine gauger and surveyor, and led a long, quiet and rather prosperous life. During his life he knew how to find time and opportunity for his manyfold investigations with microscope and knife without in any way neglecting his duty as a municipal employee. He was without an academic education and entirely self-made, but he had a natural genius for observation, together with the greatest ability in making preparations and in constructing microscopes, which he used to study known and unknown living beings. After his investigations received international fame, he himself became an international tourist attraction. Even Czar Peter took a look at him and his work when he travelled through Delft on his canal yacht. Van Leeuwenhoek, so we read, answered Peter's invitation to visit him "and had the honor of showing him, among other remarkable discoveries, through his particular glasses the marvelous circulation in the tail of an eel, which so delighted the prince that in these and other contemplations he spent no less than two hours". (From a description of 1731.) Peter had already picked up some anatomical knowledge from Professor Ruysch in Amsterdam and was therefore not unprepared. Such a visit did not turn van Leeuwenhoek's head at all; he went on working undisturbed and quietly in his Delft house as long as he lived, engaged in microscopic research till he died in 1723, more than ninety years old.

Van Leeuwenhoek used lenses that he ground himself, following a procedure that he did not disclose and discovered a world of microscopic creatures even in such innocuous places as a drop of water from the nearby Berkel Lake. Up to now man had only known of his own world and of the plants and animals that he could see with the naked eye. And he also knew of the "macrocosmos", the world of the solar system and the stars of which, just in this last part of the seventeenth century, the enormous dimensions became better known and understood through the computation of the solar parallax by Huygens' contemporaries at the French Academy. Now came van Leeuwenhoek and proved the existence of an unsuspected microcosmos of which the infusoria, microscopically small creatures of one cell living in water and discovered by him, turned out to be only a tiny part. Van Leeuwenhoek, therefore, is the founder of microbiology and even bacteriology, because he knew how to construct microscopes with a (linear) enlargement of 200 or more, even as is believed, of 400 to 500 or more. This gave him the opportunity to describe creatures that we now call bacteria. He also moved into the territory of Swammerdam whom he personally knew and studied the anatomy of insects; "a fly", he describes, "has more than 100, nay more than 1,000 eyes, the silk worm has 6,236 facets in the eye, they are hexagonal, and a dragon fly has in every cornea 12,544 facets". He extended the attention to botany and discovered details of the structure of plants such as transport canals. He contributed to the knowledge of the circulation of the blood of humans and animals, described how the blood moves in the capillaries and investigated blood corpuscles. An extensive investigation was devoted to the flea. He described the metamorphosis from egg to larva, from larva to cocoon and from cocoon to adult insects and contradicted decisively the traditional view that such animals as the flea were generated out of rotting material or even floor dust. He understood that they were fertilized in the same way as was the case with higher animals. On the larva of a flea he saw mites, parasites on a parasite. Later on Jonathan Swift made a little ditty on this fact, one we can quote this time without scruples:

> So naturalists observe, a flea
> Has smaller fleas that on him
> prey

And these have smaller fleas to
bite them,
And so proceed ad infinitum
(1733).

This is a paraphrase of the food chain that van Leeuwenhoek extended: larger animals eat smaller ones, and the last link are the bacteria. And so he was on occasion an ecologist — the number of sciences with modern names to which he contributed is considerable indeed.

All these discoveries, and we have only indicated a few of them, were faithfully communicated to the Royal Society in London in his pleasant everyday Dutch (he did not know any other language). Many of these letters were published by the Society in the English language. It was his Delft townsman Reinier de Graaf who established van Leeuwenhoek's connection with the Royal Society, and his first publication dates from the year of his introduction, 1673. From this date till van Leeuwenhoek's death these letters traveled regularly to London; more than two hundred are known. Between 1684 and 1718 many of these were published in separate volumes, in Dutch as well as in Latin. In 1939 a beginning was made to publish "all the letters" as completely as possible, and nine volumes have already appeared. It is also worthwhile to have a look at the microscopes of van Leeuwenhoek, several of which have been preserved. They are small enough to be kept in the palm of one's hand, with two small metal plates, usually of copper, with a small glass sphere as a lens placed between them and with a movable pin and screws for placing an object. Despite the simplicity of these instruments, they surpassed in magnifying power almost all simple and compound microscopes till the beginning of the nineteenth century. It is impossible to conceal our admiration for the way in which this modest man from Delft, one of the greatest naturalists of all times, knew how to discover a whole new world with simple, if sophisticated, tools. Let us listen to his own words for a moment. In a much quoted letter of September 17, 1683 he describes what we now recognize as bacteria in the matter he scraped off his own teeth. First he says that he keeps his teeth very clean

yet notwithstanding, my teeth are not so cleaned thereby, but what there sticketh or groweth between some of my front ones and my grinders (whenever I inspected them with a magnifying mirror), a little white matter, which was as thick as if it were batter. On examining this, I judged (albeit I could discern not a-moving in it) that there yet were living animalcules therein. I have therefore mixed it, at divers times, with clean rain-water (in which there were no animalcules), and also with spittle, that I took out of my mouth, after ridding it of air-bubbles (lest the bubbles should make any motion in the spittle): and I then most always saw, with great wonder, that in this said matter there were many very little living animalcules, very prettily a-moving.

Van Leeuwenhoek showed in a drawing that he had seen, and distinguished between several types. His information is precise enough to allow modern bacteriologists to determine the modern names of these "little animals". To indicate their dimension he wrote: "I imagined I could see a good thousand of them in a quantity of material that was no bigger than a hundredth of a sand-grain". If we estimate the diameter of a grain of sand to be half a millimeter then a simple calculation shows that the bacteria with a length of about one thousandth of a millimeter have room enough to move very prettily.

6

With Swammerdam, de Graaf and van Leeuwenhoek we have met three Dutch scientists who made major contributions to the understanding of the reproductive process of men and animal. We can add Steno to them and also two English scientists, William Harvey and Jeremiah Grew. As in the case of the circulation of the blood, it was Harvey who took the initiative. In a publication of 1651 on the generation of animals of which the content is often summarized in the motto *omnia ex ovo*, that is, every living being has come from an egg, he moved a tremendous step ahead. Only eighty years earlier Volcher Koyter had restricted himself to the study of the development of the chicken from the egg. Nehemiah Grew made an important contribution to the knowledge of the generation of plants, seeing in the stamens the male organs of the plant. In the fact that the pollen must come to the pistils to produce fruit he saw an analogy with the fertilization process of animals. Swammerdam, followed by van Leeuwenhoek, stressed the organic development of the animal from the embryo and from the egg. Where Harvey had, in some cases, still postulated "spontaneous generation" from mud and rotting matter, these Dutchmen denied the possibility of such spontaneous generation. De Graaf, in his study on the generative organs of man and higher animals, gave a very accurate description of the structure of these organs. Van Leeuwenhoek subjected the male sperm − the so-called spermatozoa − to a microscopic investigation, but mentioned that a new creature developed from the spermatozoa and that the female body is only a "receiving vessel": an interesting reflection of male chauvinism in the biological sciences.

This whole topic is full of sociological and philosophical elements; the fact itself that it was tackled without hesitation shows how two centuries of modern research had expanded scientific vision. But even Linnaeus, when he published in 1735 and later, his sexual classification of plants (his ideas came to fruition in Clifford's garden near Haarlem) had to hear that his classification based on numbers of stamens and pistils was offensive to delicate feelings and, in truth, was indecent. The theory of Swammerdam that the adult develops organically from the embryo and the

embryo similarly from egg and seed cell was a generalization from
his observation "that all limbs of a pupa and also of a butterfly
are already lying in position in the caterpillar". This led him and
many others to the so-called theory of preformation which claims
that every new generation is generated from the surrounding in
which it is already present — so that all of us, Julius Caesar and the
Pope, Euclid and Mohammed were already encapsulated "inside the
uterus of Eve", one being inside the other and so on *ad infinitum*.
This interesting mechanical theory, which made a biological explanation of hereditary sin possible, was popular for a long time
and also had some influence on philosophy, for example, Leibniz's
theory of monads. Sometimes the Bible was invoked in the defense of this theory (e.g., Hebrews 7:10). Opposed to the "egg
theory" was the "spermatozoa theory" as propagated by van
Leeuwenhoek, which saw the beginning of the new creature in
the "little animals" of the male seed; some of those who espoused
this theory even believed to recognize, in the form of the spermatozoa, the adult animal or the adult human being. All these theories were in turn connected with more general ideas prevalent
at that time. Some of them go back to Aristotle, such as the
doctrine of the so-called chain of life, according to which no
intermediary forms could fail to exist in the divine plan from mite
to man. Related to this theory was the doctrine of the unity of
structure of all living creatures, a doctrine proclaiming that God
always worked in the same way. This theory was often used by
van Leeuwenhoek as a guide: a vibrating hair of a microscopical
animal from the class of infusoria was really a little leg and therefore had to have the same structure. The studies on the process
of generation of man, animal and plant were to a certain extent
guided by this theory. We must not forget that our scientists were
investigators who had learned that the experiment must decide
and even if they started their work with a preconceived theory
they were ready to obey the facts of nature. The result was great

progress in this whole field towards the end of the Golden Century and shortly afterwards, a development that only made a new leap ahead at the beginning of the nineteenth century with the discovery of the cell in plants and animals. This structure was already pointed out by van Leeuwenhoek, but its function was fully understood only at a much later time.

We should not close this chapter without mentioning Johann Rudolph Glauber, a German iatrochemist who established himself in Amsterdam in the 1640s. Here he invented furnaces for distillation that could reach high temperatures. After some years in Germany he returned to Amsterdam. He had a famous laboratory used for the preparation of all kinds of chemical preparations, among them the sodium sulphate that carries his name (Glauber's salt). He is sometimes considered the first industrial chemist. He died in 1670.

CHAPTER X

COLONIAL SCIENCE

1

Whatever our likes or dislikes concerning the political and moral aspects of the colonial system may be, there cannot be any doubt that it stimulated some good scientific work. From the beginning colonial authorities, or at any rate some of them, encouraged the activities of physicians and naturalists or undertook such work themselves. The very preparation of the voyages across the oceans required scientific advice, as we have seen in the case of Plancius and Waghenaer, and some of their pupils carried an enquiring mind with them to the countries overseas. We have already mentioned that the first voyage to East India, under the De Houtmans, was responsible for a first classification of the constellations of the Southern hemisphere, based on Pieter Dirckz. Keizer's observations from the crow's nest. Jacob de Bondt or Bontius, son of the first professor of medicine at Leiden University and founder of its hortus, arrived in Java in 1627 as physician with the expedition returning Jan Pietersz. Coen as Governor General. Through his book *De medicina Indorum* (1642) he became one of the European founders of tropical medicine. It contains many chapters on diseases Bontius had to treat, including beriberi, now known as the disease which led to the discovery of the vitamins by the Dutch bacteriologist Christiaan Eykman during his stay in Indonesia (the Dutch East Indies) around 1890. We have also mentioned the voyages of discovery undertaken by order of the Dutch Governors General, voyages leading to a better geographical understanding of East Asian coastal regions and of "Southland". Of

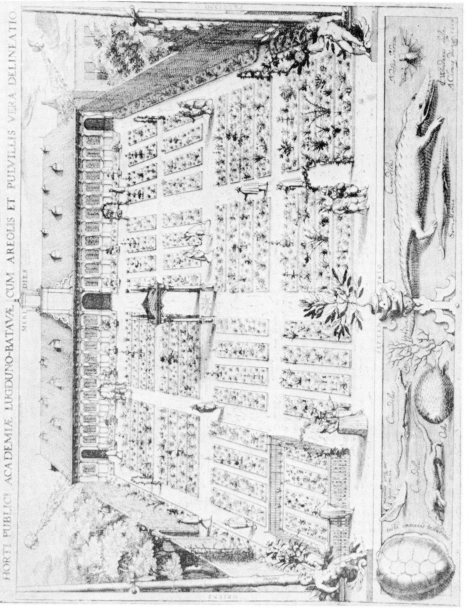

The Botanical Garden at Leiden. Engraving by J. C. Woudanus (1610) *(Museum Boerhaave, Leiden)*.

Jan Swammerdam (1637–1680). Bust by Stins (*Amsterdams Historisch Museum*).

Frederik Ruysch (1638–1731), by an unknown artist (*Amsterdam Historisch Museum*).

"Anatomical Lesson of Dr. Nicolaas Tulp", by Rembrandt (1632) (*Mauritshuis, The Hague*).

Antoni van Leeuwenhoek (1632–1723), by J. Verkolje (1686)
(*Museum Boerhaave, Leiden*).

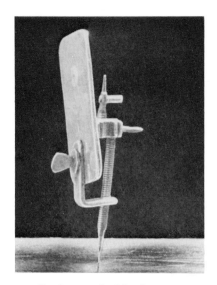

Van Leeuwenhoek's microscope
(*Museum Boerhaave, Leiden*).

A small pendulum clock by Salomon Coster (1657) – the oldest
of its kind in existence (Huygens invented the pendulum clock
in December, 1656) (*Museum Boerhaave, Leiden*).

Georg Éverhard Rumphius (1628–1702). Engraving by F. Halma from *Amboinsche Rariteitkamer* (1705) (*Museum Boerhaave, Leiden*).

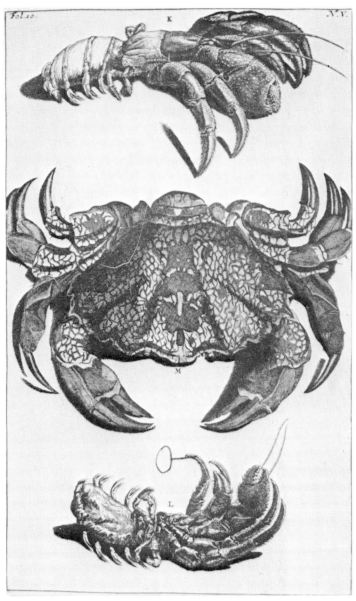

K and L: hermit crabs living in the shells of snails; M: stone crab. From
Amboinsche Rariteitkamer (1705) (*Museum Boerhaave, Leiden*).

course, we ought to be careful with the terms "discovery" and "founders", since the native peoples had discovered these countries long before the advent of the Europeans, and Indian physicians had long since studied tropical diseases. Here we shall limit our-selves to Hollanders and other Europeans in the service of the East and West India Companies and try to avoid expressions with colo-nialist overtones.

Trade and colonization were in the hands of two monopolies, the United East India Company (VOC), chartered in 1602, and the West India Company (WIC), chartered in 1621. The former controlled the Cape of Good Hope region and territories eastward in India, Ceylon (now Sri Lanka) and what we now call Indonesia. It was managed by a board of wealthy merchants, the Lords Seven-teen, and greatly enriched itself during the seventeenth century. Later it began to stagnate and was dissolved in 1798. The West India Company traded with America and the West Coast of Africa, had a short period of prosperity due mostly to piracy and slave traffic, but expired already in 1675. A resurrected body struggled on till 1791. This company was governed by the Lords Nineteen.

The WIC founded New Amsterdam in 1626 after the famous purchase by Peter Minuit (or Minnewit) of Manhattan Island for commodities worth sixty guilders (probably Karolus guilders of Charles V, weighing 2.91 grams of gold apiece). The settlement never contributed much to the arts and sciences. We have a few descriptions of the economy, ethnic composition and the natural history of the place and a few maps such as the Visscher map of 1655 with the well-known profile of New Amsterdam with fort, windmill, tavern, church and gibbet. It is said that this map and sketch was made with the assistance of a tobacco trader from Bohemia in service of the WIC, Augustus Hermann, who later made a name for himself in Maryland as cartographer, engineer and grand seigneur. In 1665, New Amsterdam, in British hands, became New York.

What we know of the early years of the Dutch in America and the WIC in general is in part due to a wealthy and learned Amsterdam merchant, Johannes de Laet, a native of Antwerp and one of the Lords Nineteen. He became known as the author of the book *Nieuwe wereldt ofte beschryvinghe van West Indien* (New World or Description of the West Indies), a stately volume on what was called, in the tradition of Pliny, the natural history of America, that is, everything worth knowing about it. De Laet never travelled across the Atlantic, but did extensive reading on whatever sources came his way, including the Spanish historiographers such as Oviedo and Acosta and the archives of the West India Company. The book appeared in 1625; an enlarged edition, as well as a Latin and a French translation were published afterwards.

The arts and sciences flourished far better in Brazil, another short-lived colony of the WIC. This was due exclusively to the personality of one man, Prince Johan Maurits of Nassau-Siegen, a cousin of the Orange *stadhouders* Maurice and Frederick Henry. From 1636 to 1644 this Nassau prince was governor of that section of Northern Brazil which the WIC had taken from the Portuguese in the present state of Pernambuco. A prince in true Renaissance tradition, Johan Maurits surrounded himself in his capital of Recife with craftsmen, painters and scientists, built up the city with a government palace, sent the painters Frans and Pieter Post into the country to make documentaries and the Leiden physician Willem Piso, assisted by the German scholar Georg Marcgraff, to study the natural history of the region in the widest sense of the word. This led to the publication of the magnificent *Historia naturalis Brasiliae* in twelve books, four with Piso's description of medicinal herbs and eight with Marcgraff's description of plants, animals and customs. The book, dedicated to Johan Maurits, appeared in 1648 after the Prince had returned to Europe and Marcgraff had died (only thirty-three years old). A second edition of the work, that belongs to the best published

on natural history in the seventeenth century, appeared in 1658
under a different title, edited by Piso more as a handbook of
tropical medicine, pharmacology and natural history, with unpub-
lished papers of Bontius added.

Piso returned with the Prince to Holland and to his medical
practice there, where he was active for thirty years as a leading
Amsterdam physician, a colleague of Tulp. In 1942 Brazil paid
off an ancient debt by publishing at São Paulo a beautiful Portuguese edition of Piso's *Historia*, with extensive commentary.

Johan Maurits built another grand Renaissance building in the
Hague, next to the house of his friend Constantijn Huygens. The
Huygens house is gone, but the Maurits house still stands and
is the famous museum, the Maurits House, where you can see
Rembrandt's 'Anatomical Lesson of Dr. Tulp'. Both buildings
were built under the supervision of Pieter Post. His brother Frans
continued as painter of tropical landscapes at Haarlem.

Of a later date are the beautiful paintings of insects by Maria
Sibylla Merian. Hailing from a German family of painters and engravers related to the Utrecht school of flower painters, she became
in 1685 associated with the sect of the Labadists at Wieuwerd at
their Frisian castle. From there she went in 1699 with her youngest
daughter to Surinam (Dutch Guiana), where the Labadists had a
colony. She stayed there till 1702, continuing her nature studies
with great perseverance despite the unhealthy climate and the fact
that she was already in her fifties. Her *Metamorphosis insectorum
Surinamesium ofte Verandering der Surinamse Insecten* appeared
in 1705 in a folio edition, a beautiful book, still famous in its
field, with its paintings of insects, caterpillar and butterfly or
moth always together with the feeding plant. These pictures are
not only of interest to entomologists and botanists, but have also
received wide admiration for their artistic merits. Their painter
died in 1717 after her return to Amsterdam.

The most remarkable students of natural history in the service of the East India Company are Jan Hendrick Adriaan van Rheede tot Drakenstein and Georg Rumphius. Van Rheede, of Utrecht nobility, climbed up rapidly in the service of the VOC and was from 1671 to 1677 governor of Malabar in the present state of Madras in India. He spent his tremendous energy in the administration of the Company and in the satisfaction of his passion to get to know the flora of this part of India. He was one of those old-time seigneurs of the sergeant-major type who knew how to teach solid respect for Dutch authority wherever he went, a driver of men when he wanted results, be they in profits for the Lords Seventeen or in additions to his growing collections. He called in the aid of Indian princes, founded an advisory college of fifteen or sixteen learned Brahmins, travelled with hundreds of native servants up the rivers to collect plants, and had native draftsmen at home to draw pictures. Some Dutchmen, amateur scientists, were at his side. Thus the groundwork was laid for his grand tome *Malabarse Cruythof* that appeared in Latin as *Hortus Indicus Malabaricus*, the first volume in 1678, followed by eleven more between that year and 1703, all beautifully illustrated. It was the first great European work with descriptions and pictures of the Indian flora, a book of considerable value even now, a magnificent monument for this energetic fellow, who also made a name for himself in Ceylon and in the Cape Colony of South Africa. The Dutch version of the *Cruythof* appeared in 1689 in two volumes; there exists an English translation of 1758 by the versatile apothecary-botanist John Hill who also prepared an English edition of Swammerdam's *Book of Nature*.

An entirely different figure is the modest Georg Everhard Rumpf or Rumphius, like Marcgraff born in Germany. In 1652, at the age of twenty-four, he entered the service of the Dutch East India company and in 1653 was sent to the island of Amboina. Here, in the capital of the Moluccas, Rumphius served the company dutifully as merchant and administrator from 1653 till his death in 1702. But this ambition was directed in a different direction. With great energy, and not assisted like van Rheede by groups of collaborators, he investigated the flora and fauna of this part of the world, adding year after year new treasures to his knowledge and drawings to his collection, bringing his results together in heavy illustrated tomes. He knew how to involve others – even some of his superiors in the company – with his enthusiasm and perseverance; the Governors General Maetsuyker and Camphuys were his friends and admirers. How beautifully Rumphius knew to describe "little horns and shells", how many additions to the collections of "rarities"! There was more, however, to this interest of so many people, including Rumphius' superiors, than a simple passion for collecting, for his enormous energy and self-sacrifice in his longing for knowledge found general admiration. He became blind, but continued, with his fingers as a substitute for his eyes. He lost his wife and youngest daughter in an earthquake, and though the repercussions lasted several years, his energies came back. The Company gave him a couple of draftsmen as assistants, and he was also aided by his son. The great work was almost finished when it was almost entirely lost in a great fire. He started again and repaired the damage. In the middle of 1692, six books of the *Amboinsch Kruidboek* were sent to Holland. The ship was wrecked together with the manuscript. But Governor General Camphuys had taken care that a copy was left in Batavia and was sent to Holland in 1696. This time it arrived safely and was followed by newer books. But although the Lords Seventeen, directors of the Company, admired the work of Rumphius and praised the author, they could not find the money to publish this expensive work. They sat on it till 1736, and the *Amboinsch Kruidboek* with Dutch and Latin text appeared between 1741 and 1750 in six folios.

Already earlier, in 1705, but also after the death of Rumphius, the *Amboinsche Rariteitkamer* was published with information on the worms, locusts, "horns and shells" of the Moluccas. His *Amboinsch Dierboek* (Book of the animals of Amboina) was never printed and the manuscript seems to be lost, but it is believed that the Reverend François Valentijn, in his five volume *Oud en Nieuw Oost Indiën* (1724–1726), used this manuscript to a considerable extent. Much of what Rumphius had written on botany and zoology, but also on mineralogy, zoology and palae-ontology remains of direct scientific significance, and the works of the "blind seer of Amboina" are still being consulted by the specialists. Recently his name was again mentioned in connection with the medicine, Rauwolfia, used in psychopharmacology.

In 1902 the Colonial Museum in Haarlem paid tribute to his memory with a beautiful volume. His grave is on Amboina. This quiet and tireless worker, who was daunted neither by the climate that robbed him of his eyesight, nor the fire that consumed his work, nor the earth that destroyed his family, nor the water that took his manuscripts, belongs to all who love the nature of the tropics. He belongs both to the Netherlands and to Indonesia.

2

The relations between the East India Company and Japan also resulted in work of scientific importance. From 1641 onwards the Company had a depot (*faktorij*) on the island of Deshima (Decima) near Nagasaki and here several European scientists were able to obtain some understanding of Japan, just as Japanese scientists could acquire some understanding about what happened in Europe. One of these scientists was Engelbert Kämpfer, a physician from Westphalia who entered the service of the Company in 1684 as a medical man. He wrote a well-known book on Japan, where he lived from 1690 to 1692. This *Beschrijving van Japan* (Description of Japan) also appeared in English, French and

German. Among the many interesting things described in this book we find the now so famous acupuncture which the Japanese took over from China. The commercial depot on the island was continued until 1854. Deshima is no longer an island, but has become part of Nagasaki.

Seventeenth-century Dutchmen also did scientific work in Africa and West Asia. A man from Amsterdam, Olfert Dapper, traveled widely in Europe, Asia and Africa and described his experience in works of which *Naukeurige beschrijvinge der Afrikaansche eylanden* (1676) (Exact description of the African regions and the African islands) is perhaps best remembered. The book deals with countries in West Africa. Dapper also published a historical description of Amsterdam (1663). In his book on Asia (1680) we find a pretty picture of the tower of Babel as it was imagined at that time.

CHAPTER XI

INTO THE AGE OF BOERHAAVE

With Ruysch, Witsen, Merian, van Leeuwenhoek and Rumphius we have already left the Golden Century behind us and have entered the period we can associate with Herman Boerhaave, the Leiden professor of medicine. This "Age of Boerhaave" was no Golden Century and the Regents were no longer the sturdy "boys of Jan De Witt" deciding on the fate of Europe. Yet the age should not be underestimated. It was not only the time of overfed rentiers living on their investments in their town houses and country homes along rivers like the Vecht with their formal gardens, arbors and pretty vistas, a maximum of obsequious poor on charity and a minimum of picturesque sea dogs. It was also a time of continued scientific life at the universities, especially those of Leiden and Utrecht, and though contributions to exact science diminished in value after Huygens' death in 1695 and the departure of Johann Bernoulli from Groningen in 1705, medicine, experimental physics, botany and chemistry flourished and attracted students from all over the world.

This shift of emphasis shows that the temper of academic learning had changed. The Cartesianism of the seventeenth century had lost much of its dogmatic and speculative character and had given way to greater appreciation of testing, of experimenting. Where the historians of art speak of the change from classicism to baroque, the philosophers of the change from Metaphysics to Enlightenment, the historians of science can speak of a change from Cartesianism to experimental philosophy. Newton became the new hero.

One of the harbingers of the Enlightenment delivered his

message from Rotterdam. Pierre Bayle, a refugee Huguenot and a Calvinist minister, settled here in 1681. Among his many literary and philosophical writings his *Dictionaire historique et critique* (1697) stands out, an enormously erudite plea for reason and tolerance mixed with a touch of ironic scepticism toward tradition and what he saw as superstition. Another earlier book, the *Pensées diverses sur le comète* (1682) attacked the belief in the ominous portent of comets, but is mainly remembered by Bayle's contention that an atheist can be as moral as a Christian. This all made Bayle's life far from easy, and he lost his position as a teacher in Rotterdam. A similar fate befell another Calvinist minister, like Bayle influenced by Cartesianism, also a writer denouncing all this talk about comets foretelling disaster — like Bayle he was stirred into action by the appearance of a spectacular comet, fiery in the starry winter nights of late 1680. This minister was Balthasar Bekker, with a flock first in Franeker, then, after 1679, in Amsterdam. Unpopular already for his position on comets, he became a marked man when during 1691—1693 he published his three volume *De betoverde wereld* (the world bewitched), a powerful attack on theological grounds for the belief in the workings of demons, witches and warlocks, still held in many a Protestant and Catholic mind, though witch trials in the Republic had already ceased after 1610.[1] Bekker did not deny the existence of the Devil, but, as has been said, banned the Devil into Hell. The book cost him his job, but the Amsterdam magistrate took care that he kept his salary until his death in 1698. There were translations of the book, or parts of it, into French, English and German. The book, widely discussed in the United Provinces, may have helped more than that of his predecessor Wier in undermining belief in witches in orthodox circles. But though there were no trials, belief continued and until deep in the eighteenth century persons suspected of witchcraft let themselves be weighed in the *Heksenwaag* in Oudewater, still functioning for the edification of tourists.

Boerhaave, born in 1668, became *lector* in medicine at Leiden in 1701, professor of medicine and botany in 1709 and in 1718 also of chemistry. Praising Hippocrates for his case studies, Newton and Boyle for their empirical methods, he taught, till his death in 1738, in accordance with the principles of the experimental philosophy. Of importance were also two younger men, W. J. 's Gravesande and Petrus van Musschenbroek, the latter a nephew of Simon, the instrument maker (see Chapter VIII), both professors at Leiden (Petrus for many years at Utrecht). 's Gravesande, during 1715 — 1716, was in personal contact with Newton and other members of the Royal Society in London and became one of the leading interpreters of Newtonianism in Europe. Boerhaave, not only a physician and chemist, but also a naturalist, had his correspondents all over the world, exchanging medical advice, literature, seeds and specimens in the atmosphere of goodwill and meditation typical of that period in the circles of scientists and amateurs. Boerhaave's colleague J. F. Gronovius, botanist and physician, published one of the first floras of North America, the *Flora virginica* (1739, 2nd ed. 1762). Linnaeus, Swedenborg, von Haller, Lamettrie were among those coming to the Republic for study purposes. Linnaeus published the first draft of his system, the *Systema Naturae*, in 1735 while working near Haarlem in the botanical garden of the banker George Clifford. During the first quarter of the eighteenth century Leiden counted more than two hundred foreigners among its nine hundred students.

Dutch publishers continued to print learned books in the sciences, in philology and other fields. Works that for political or theological reasons could not be published in the land where they were written, found publishers in the Republic, even Lamettrie's *L'homme machine* (1748). And although the Republic had lost its leading position among the European powers, when Adam Smith in 1776, with his *Wealth of Nations*, introduced theoretically the

new capitalist era, he spoke of "the present grandeur of Holland".
It appears that he looked at Holland with almost as much respect
as William Petty a hundred years before.[2]

NOTES

CHAPTER I

[1] The term 'Dutch Republic' was not used at that time. The expression used was 'United Provinces' or 'United Netherlands'. There was no formal constitution except the document signed in 1579 at the Union of Utrecht establishing a loose combination of seven provinces, each maintaining its own autonomy. This Union of Utrecht, somewhat amplified by a few other agreements, remained in force till 1795, when it was replaced by the so-called Batavian Republic.

[2] Gerard Kinckhuyzen (1630–1679), a school teacher in Haarlem, wrote among others an *Algebra ofte Stelkonst*. The Latin translation by Newton was never published.

[3] From a eulogy on his beloved town by the poet Joost van den Vondel. The crown was bestowed on Amsterdam by the Emperor Maximilian. Look at it, when you visit Amsterdam: it is on top of the Westertoren.

[4] Door split horizontally in two, so that the upper part opened separately; this allowed husband and wife to chat with their neighbors and the husband to smoke his long clay pipe in the open, all without getting their feet wet in the rain.

CHAPTER II

[1] Amerigo Vespucci (1451–1512) was an Italian discoverer in Spanish service. His travelogue on the *New World*, as he called it, gave the German geographer Martin Waldseemüller the idea to give the name America to this *mundus novus* (1507).

[2] Averroës (1126–1198), Latin name for the Spanish-Moroccan philosopher Ibn-Rushd.

[3] Maimonides (1135?–1204), also Moses ben Maimon, lived first in Spain, then became physician to Sultan Saladin in Cairo.

[4] Thomas Aquinas (1225–1274), Italian Dominican, theologist and philosopher known as "Doctor Angelicus".

[5] See D'Arcy W. Thompson, *On Aristotle as Biologist* (Oxford 1911).

[6] The first printed edition of the *Elements* (in the medieval Latin version of Campanus of Novara) was by Radolt in Venice, 1482. Better editions, also in the original Greek (1533), followed during the sixteenth century, in which also many other scientific texts from antiquity became available in Latin editions.

CHAPTER III

[1] Omar Khayyam (1048?–1131?), also Al-Khayyami, was a Persian mathematician and astronomer and also an Aristotelian philosopher. He is best known in the Occident for the Rubaiyat (quatrains) in the very free English version of Edward Fitzgerald (1859).

[2] Serveto was not brought to the stake because he attacked Galen, but because he expressed doubts about the Trinity.

[3] Willem Barendsz. (ca. 1550–1597) was a Dutch sailor and cartographer born on the island of Terschelling. He published (see Chapter IV), in cooperation with Plancius, a book of maps about the Mediterranean. The objects found in the ruins of Barendsz. house on Novaya Zemlya in 1871 and 1876 are in the Rijksmuseum in Amsterdam.

[4] When we write π for the ratio of circumference to diameter of the circle, we use a symbol only accepted in the eighteenth century through the authority of Leonhard Euler.

CHAPTER IV

[1] Anicius Manlius Severinus Boethius (ca. 480–524/525), Latin philosopher, mathematician and theologian, of ancient Roman aristocracy, collected in his works some of the antique scientific, philosophical and musical heritage. For many centuries he served as a source of encyclopedic learning and instruction in the arts of the *quadrivium*: arithmetic, geometry, astronomy and music.

[2] The oldest known book of this kind published in the Netherlands is from 1508, printed in Brussels, see Smeur, p. 10.

[3] In the Republic, under Protestant domination, the reform was introduced in steps between 1582 and 1701 (Great Britain and its colonies followed in 1752, when September 2 became September 15, not without some trouble here and there), Russia followed only in 1918.

[4] The use of patronymics without acceptance of a hereditary family name was not unusual in the Netherlands, so that Claes Pietersz. (Pieterszoon) may have been the son of Pieter Jansz. and father of Pieter Claesz. Better known

or affluent persons affected a family name, like De Witt or Huygens — itself
originally a patronymic: son of Hugh.

5 There already existed sea charts in Holland before Waghenaer, for instance,
a *Caerte van Oostland* (map of the Baltic) by Cornelis Anthonisz. (1543).
There also existed so-called *leeskaerten* (maps for reading), sometimes with
figures that tried to identify a land like the island of Terschelling by means
of a profile drawing.

6 This book, *Historie Naturael ende Morael van de Westersche Indien* (1598,
794 pp.), was the translation of a book written by the learned Jesuit José
Acosta who worked in Spanish America from 1570 till 1586. It was the
Historia natural y moral, 'historia natural', natural history, in the classical
sense of Pliny, that is, a description of everything worth noticing in nature, the
universe, the earth, geography, ethnology, botany, zoology, mineralogy, etc.
Acosta was particularly worried about the impact all these novelties from the
New World could have on our belief in Scripture. So, for instance, the belief
that all human beings, hence also Indians, descend from Adam and Eve, or
that all larger animals in America descend from their ancestors in Noah's
ark (insects offered no difficulty, since they were supposed to have been
produced asexually out of mud). Such difficulties and Acosta's proposed
solutions also agitated Protestant theologians, among them some in the
Netherlands.

7 Meer Afbreuk heeft ghedaan den Paus en Spaengien snoot/Met Preken ende
Ra'en dan een Heyrleger groot.

8 Calvinist preachers, denied the use of the churches in town, gathered the
faithful in open spaces outside the city gates. These were the *hageprekers*.

9 Two ships with Barendsz. as scientific leader set out in May 1596 in an
attempt to force the North-East Passage. Caught in the ice near Nova Zembla
(as the Dutch called the island), the crew had to pass the winter in this place
under severe hardships. In June 1597 the men tried to return home in two
sloops. Most of them succeeded, but Barendsz. died on the way. This adven-
ture is described in detail by Gerrit de Veer, one of the crew, in a book republished by the Linschoten company (1917). Dutch schoolchildren learn of
it through a sentimental epic written in stately alexandrines by the Rotterdam
poet Hendrik Tollens (1819).

10 Letter from Marie F. Harper, Reference Librarian, The Rhode Island
Historical Society, Providence, R. I.

11 Eratosthenes (third century B.C.) of Alexandria was one of the founders
of scientific geography. *Batavus* was the Latin name the learned Dutchman
liked to give himself after a Germanic tribe in the Rhine delta mentioned by
Roman authors and known for its courage. Another Latin name was *Belgae*
and *Belgica*, later adopted by the South Netherlanders for their kingdom.

12 The results of Snellius and those of s' Gravesande have been subjected by

N. D. Haasbroek to a modern critical examination. (See our bibliography.) A Rhineland rod was 3.767 meters.

[13] Drebbel has remained a figure of interest. After Dr. H. A. Naber, a teacher in Hoorn, in his popular booklet *De ster van 1572* (1907) had given an admiring description of the man and his work, he reproduced, around 1924, on a small scale many of Drebbel's experiments. Drebbel also made a map of Alkmaar (1597).

[14] 'Adieu, Bartjes, ik wil zwijgen
D'wijl ghij gaat ten Hemel stijgen.
'k Wenschte dat ik hier in schijn
Slechts mocht uwen Echo zijn.'

CHAPTER V

[1] The States Bible (*Statenbijbel*) was composed by a team of orthodox Calvinist ministers between 1626 and 1635, financed and authorized by the States General of the Republic. The English translation made at the direction of King James I was published in 1611. Both translations, like the Luther Bible in Germany, had great influence on the spoken and written language.

[2] Preface to the *Thiende* (1585) in the English translation by R. Norton (1608).

[3] John Napier (1550—1617), also named Neper, was a Scottish laird, ardent Calvinist, who introduced the logarithms in two books of 1614 and 1619, but not yet in the modern form with basis 10, introduced by the London professor Henry Briggs. Decimal fractions with decimal signs (period or comma) were first systematically introduced in the English translation of Napier's book of 1614 by the English mathematician Edward Wright and then were taken over by Napier himself in a book of 1617.

[4] The sailing chariot had long been known in China and is mentioned in Dutch books of Stevin's time, e.g., in Linschooten's *Itinerario* of 1596 (see Chapter IV). It is very well possible that Stevin picked up his information from this book. His sailing chariot with Prince Maurice and company, among them the seventeen year old Hugo Grotius (who later wrote about it in Latin verse), sailed along the beach from Scheveningen to Putten in less than two hours with the wind, a distance of about eighty kilometers. This must have been in 1600 or 1601. This trip by sailing chariot was frequently repeated, certainly till 1790. Sailing chariots are even now sometimes used on beaches and as "prairie schooners" they are mentioned in the U.S. during the nineteenth century. There are also sailing yachts to slide on ice. There is even more evidence indicating that Stevin took notice of contacts of his day between Western Europe and China. We think of his music theory based on the so-called duodecimal equal temperament that was also known to the Chinese

− and, after all, the Chinese had known the decimal fractions for hundreds of years in a notation that reminds us of that of Stevin. But there is not the slightest published evidence of Chinese contact in the case of music and arithmetic. For the sailing chariot see R. J. Forbes' introduction to Volume 5 of the *Principal Works of Simon Stevin* (Amsterdam 1966), pp. 3−8.

5 "Miracle and is no miracle", a motto appearing on the title page of his *Weeghconst*.

6 Ubbo Emmius (1547−1625) or Ubbo van Embden was, in 1614, the first rector of the newly founded University of Groningen. He was a member of the committee that produced the States Bible. Later on he seems to have become more tolerant and recommended the study of the three different planetary systems (Ptolemaic, Copernican, Tycho) without drawing partisan conclusions. Sibrandus Lubbertus became in 1585 professor at Franeker. He was also a militant Counter-Remonstrant and took part in the Dordrecht synod of 1619 that expelled the Remonstrants. Emmius was an able historian of Frisian history, on which he wrote a work in six volumes.

CHAPTER VI

1 Labadists were followers of the French clergyman Jean de Labadie (1610−1674). Dismissed as Walloon (i.e., French Belgian) minister at Middelburg (1699), he founded a growing community of religious-communist character at Amsterdam. Meeting with opposition, he went with about fifty followers to Herford and later to Altona near Hamburg where he died. For a while the Labadists also had colonies in Surinam and in New Jersey. (See Chapter IX.)

2 "Gommer en Armijn te hoof/dongen naar het recht geloof". F. Gomarus (1563−1641) and Jacobus Arminius (1560−1609) were both professors of theology at Leiden, when they engaged in a dispute about predestination. Arminius preached a more tolerant Deity, his followers, after a "Remonstrantie" presented 1610 to the States of Holland, were called Remonstrants. They still exist, still representing a liberal, "latitudinarian" religious position, analogous to Unitarianism. Gomarus defended orthodox Calvinism: God's eternal resolution to give eternal bliss to some and leave others in damnation. Plancius accused the Arminians of Pelagianism.

3 At the end of the century we find Balthasar Bekker and Pierre Bayle, see Chapter XI.

4 The oldest-known book on dikes and drainages in the Netherlands is that of Andries Vierlingh, *Tractaet van dijckagie* (Treatise on Dykage) (1570). The manuscript without drawings was rediscovered in 1895 and printed in 1920 in The Hague. Stevin wrote much about locks and mills, also in connection with fortification.

5 According to De Roever (see bibliography) Leeghwater's merits have been grossly overestimated. He was essentially a builder of windmills, not an engineer, and his plan for the draining of the Haarlem Lake was no good at all. Far better was the plan by Jacob Bartelsz. Veeris, also of 1641. Veeris' merits — De Roever calls him, in contrast to Leeghwater, a "masterful hydraulic expert" — have been neglected in the light of the "Leeghwater legend".

6 As Mr. E. van Gelder, city librarian of Veurne, kindly informs me, there is till a stone mill in operation from Cobergher's time. Built in 1620, it is now run by electricity, but in the future will be driven by wind power.

7 Most windmills disappeared in the nineteenth century. In 1900 there were still 4,000, around 1960 only 1,000. During the last fifty years societies have been formed to preserve what is left. The water mills for paper manufacture have disappeared except for one overshot mill now performing at the Open Air Museum near Arnhem. One windpapermill is still in business near the Zaan, built in 1692.

8 There is much more to say about this capitalist spirit, with its "time is money", and its influence on certain domestic virtues as thrift and economy, especially in the formative period of capitalism. W. Sombart, the Berlin sociologist and economist, gave thought to this, see, e.g., his book *Der Bourgeois* (1913).

CHAPTER VII

1 Marin Mersenne (1588–1648) was a Minorite Franciscan. Through personal contact and correspondence he was one of the founders of the European scientific community that began to develop in the seventeenth century and led to the foundation of academies, scientific societies and periodicals. To this circle belonged Gassendi or Pierre Gassend (1592–1655), French philosopher, clergyman and man of science.

2 The mercantilist doctrines held by European statesmen of the seventeenth and eighteenth centuries, such as Colbert under Louis XIV, were characterized by great stress on gold and silver as the principal sources of prosperity of a state and by stressing trade monopolies under state charters such as the East India Company. With the industry still in an early capitalist stage the stress was mainly on trade, especially trans-Atlantic and Asian trade.

3 This American theologian/mathematician was Josiah Meigs (1757–1822), first professor at Yale University, later president of the University of Georgia.

CHAPTER VIII

1 An Athenaeum was an institution for advanced education, though not

quite as advanced as a university, but more advanced than a Latin school. The Athenaea founded during the seventeenth century in the Republic were also called Illustrious Schools. There were Athenaea in Amsterdam, Dordrecht, Deventer, Breda and some other places. The Athenaeum in Amsterdam, founded in 1632, became a university in 1876.

2 The three body problem is the following: to derive from the equations of Newton the motions of three moving bodies under the influence of their mutual attraction. The system sun-moon-earth is such a system of three bodies. The theoretical, mathematical solution is extremely difficult. At present, in problems of space missiles, computers are used.

3 It is remarkable that many of these unorthodox and often free-thinking sects have influenced or have been influenced by men and women of scientific leaning. We think of the collegians and Spinoza, of Madame de Bourignon and Swammerdam, the Labadists and van Deventer and Maria Merian. This reminds us of the Jansenists in France who counted Antoine Arnauld and Blaise Pascal, both mathematicians and philosophers, among their friends and later of the Quakers in England and Pennsylvania who had great influence on the development of science and industry. Incidentally, the Jansenists, those "Calvinist Catholics" as they have been called, owed their name to a Dutch Catholic theologian, Cornelius Jansen, who, during the last years before his death in 1630, was bishop of Ieper (Ypres) in the Southern Netherlands. They had considerable influence in that region, where Arnauld himself went in 1679 to avoid persecution and where he died (in Brussels, 1694). He was co-author of the widely studied "Logique de Port-Royal" (1660), a logic written under Cartesian influence and with ideas on probability and other subjects interesting for the study of Pascal, and for the origins of the mathematical theory of probability.

4 Nicolaas Hartsoeker (1656–1725), a native of Gouda, was an instrument maker (microscopes and other sophisticated tools) and lens grinder. He accompanied Huygens to the observatory in Paris, tutored Czar Peter in Amsterdam during 1697 and was from 1704 to 1716 professor at the University of Düsseldorf, then under the Electorate of the Palatinate. He was also an embryologist.

Samuel van Musschenbroek (1639–1681) belonged to a family of brass casters and instrument makers at Leiden. Samuel made air pumps, microscopes and other instruments. His nephew Petrus (1692–1761), a professor in Utrecht, then in Leiden, became a famous leader of the so-called experimental philosophy of the eighteenth century.

CHAPTER IX

1 Of these universities those at Franeker and Harderwijk have ceased to exist.

Napoleon took care of that. The kingdom of the Netherlands, founded in 1815, maintained the remaining three. In the later part of the nineteenth and during the twentieth century several more institutes for higher education were established.

2 The Amsterdam hall where the anatomical lesson took place, the *Theatrum anatomicum*, did not belong to the Athenaeum, but to the surgeons' guild that only through Tulp began to have a scientific character. Before this time surgeons and barbers belonged to the same guild. A physician with a university degree had a much higher social position than a surgeon and was very conscious of it. This Amsterdam hall was first in the *Vleeshal* in the Nes, but in Tulp's days had been moved to the St. Anthony's *Waag* (Weighing Hall), where it stayed from 1619 to 1639. It may interest our reader that in Rembrandt's painting we know not only the names of all participating students, but even the name of the corpse.

3 He is even mentioned in Laurence Sterne's *Tristram Shandy* (1759) where we also find a reference to Stevin.

4 A contemporary writes that as a result of a busy practice Tulp "was forced to ride a coach drawn by a horse, having under his house on the Keizersgracht west of the Westerkerk prepared a place for it in the basement".

5 The expression orangutan is Malay for 'forest man' and was used for many years as a general expression for primates. Tulp's orangutan must have been a gorilla or chimpanzee; the ape of the Englishman Edward Tyson in his *Orang-Outang sive homo silvestris* of 1699 has been, it seems, recognized as a chimpanzee.

6 He should not be confused with Jacobus Sylvius (Jacques Dubois, 1478– 1555), physician and teacher of anatomy in Paris, teacher of Vesalius whose later anti-Galenism he opposed.

7 Experiments with muzzled dogs and other animals were performed on living animals. This torture was sometimes defended with the Cartesian dictum that animals are after all only automata. We should not forget, however, that the surgeons also had to cut humans in the living flesh, even though they tried to diminish the pain by serving some sleep-inducing, narcotic or alcoholic drink. Pain belonged to the life of our ancestors as pollution belongs to ours, but we do not believe that the latter is a visitation by God.

8 One of Sylvius' pupils was Cornelis Bontekoe (1640–1688) known as the 'tea doctor' because of the high praise he bestowed on tea as a panacea. This was the period in which tobacco, coffee, tea and cocoa found gradual acceptance in Western Europe, tobacco already in the second half of the sixteenth century, also as a panacea against different maladies. Among the authors in Holland who first mentioned these products are Clusius and van Linschoten. Gouda, we have seen, became famous for its clay pipe manufacture; we see

the good Dutchmen smoking their pipes on the paintings of Jan Steen and Adriaen Brouwer.

9 This is based on a note of Dr. Gunter Mann in *Sudhoffs Archiv für Geschichte der Medizin* (1961), pp. 176–178. The story of these drinking Russian sailors had already been told by nobody less than Cuvier (1841) and has since been repeated in a number of serious works.

10 When Clusius came to Leiden he was more than sixty years old and too weak for much garden work, so that the actual Hortulanus was the apothecary Dirck Cluyt. A laburnum planted in 1601 is still flowering every year, or so we read in a guide of 1963. This Hortus is one of the oldest in Europe. The oldest is that of Padua, of 1543.

11 In Vienna Clusius made the acquaintance of the learned Flemish Nobleman Ogier de Busbecq, imperial ambassador at Constantinople. De Busbecq travelled widely and helped Clusius to many seeds, bulbs and plants unknown to Western and Central Europe. They were first sent to Vienna and then to Leiden. Among them were the tulip, the lilac, the horse chestnut, the gladiolus, the sycamore and the calamus. We know that there was a red tulip flowering in Augsburg in 1559. Clusius forwarded his seeds, bulbs and plants again to colleagues and friends. Some years ago the introduction of the tulip into Holland was commemorated with a festive parade from Istanbul through Europe to the Netherlands.

For the relationship between Clusius, Dodonaeus, de Busbecq and other Netherlanders at the Prague-Viennese court of Rudolph II and the Antwerp circle around Ortelius and Plantin see Nicolette Mout, *Acta Historiae Neerlandicae 9* (1976) 1–30.

12 The *Commelina communis*, of Asian origin, is the common day flower of North America. The blue flowers have three petals, two big ones and a small one. This, said Linnaeus, who in his own way liked a little joke, remined him of the Commelins, two of them were great botanists, but the third was only a small one.

13 Niels Stensen (1638–1686), a Dane, studied in Amsterdam with Blasius and in Leiden with Sylvius between 1660 and 1663. After that he went to other countries. Originally a Lutheran, he became a Catholic and later even a bishop. He did fundamental work not only as a physiologist but also as a geologist.

CHAPTER XI

1 No witch was burned in the Northern Netherlands after 1597, a remarkable tribute to the 'Erasmian' attitude of many magistrates. Persecutions of witches continued in the surrounding countries, including the Southern Netherlands,

all through the seventeenth century. In Calvinist Scotland the last witch was burned in 1727.

2 Those readers who would like to find out more about science in the Republic during the first half of the eighteenth century, will find a good introduction in the book by G. A. Lindeboom, *Herman Boerhaave, the Man and His Work* (London, 1968). See also the article by W. D. Hackman in our bibliography.

BIBLIOGRAPHY

I. SOME LITERATURE IN ENGLISH

A short survey of the history of the Northern Netherlands was written by A. J. Barnouw, *the Making of Modern Holland* (New York, 1944). Another survey, but now only on the Golden Age, in K. H. D. Haley, *The Dutch in the Seventeenth Century* (London, New York, 1972) with beautiful illustrations and a section on science.

The standard history is P. J. Blok, *History of the People of the Netherlands* (5 vols., New York, 1898–1912). It can be supplemented, with a different outlook, by P. Geyl, *The Netherlands in the Seventeenth Century* (2 vols., New York, 1961, 1964) and B. H. M. Vlekke, *Evolution of the Dutch Nation* (New York, 1945, reprinted 1963 in the Netherlands).

It is still a pleasure to read in the somewhat dated books by the Yankee historian J. L. Motley, *The Rise of the Dutch Republic* (3 vols., New York, 1856), followed by six other volumes (1860–1874), written to illustrate, as Motley saw it, the struggle between freedom and tyranny, comparing the Dutch and the American struggles for independence.

The work of Galileo, Bacon, Descartes, Huygens, Newton, together with that of their predecessors in the Middle Ages and Antiquity is investigated with scrupulous care in E. J. Dijksterhuis, *The Mechanization of the World Picture* (Oxford, 1961; translated from the Dutch edition of 1950). Shorter is A. R. Hall, *The Scientific Revolution 1500–1800* (London, etc., 1954).

Biographical and bibliographical data on many Dutch scientists are found in the fourteen volumes of the *Dictionary of Scientific Biography* (New York, 1970–1978).

Here follow some monographs:

Bell, A. E., *Christian Huygens and the Development of Science in the Seventeenth Century*. London, 1947.
Bowen, H. H., *John De Witt, Grandpensionary of Holland*. Princeton, N.J., 1978, esp. Ch. 20: 'The Unphilosophical Cartesians'.
Coolidge, J. L., *The Mathematics of Great Amateurs*. Oxford, 1949. This book has a chapter on De Witt.

147

Cross, W. R., 'Dutch Cartographers of the Seventeenth Century', *Geographical Review* 5 (1918), 66–70.

Dobell, C., *Antony van Leeuwenhoek and His 'Little Animals'*. London, Amsterdam, 1932, 2nd ed. New York, 1958.

Dijksterhuis, E. J., *Simon Stevin, Science in the Netherlands around 1600*. The Hague, 1970, concise version of the Dutch edition of 1943 by R. Hooykaas and M. G. J. Minnaert.

Haasbroek, N. D., *Gemma Frisius, Tycho Brahe and Snellius and Their Triangulation*. Delft, 1968.

Hackman, W. D., 'The Growth of Science in the Netherlands in the Seventeenth and Early Eighteenth Centuries'. In M. Crossland (ed.), *The Emergence of Science in Western Europe*. New York, 1976.

Heckscher, W. S., *Rembrandt's Anatomy of Dr. Nicolas Tulp: An Iconological Study*. New York, 1950.

Hooykaas, R., 'Science and Reformation', *Journal of World History* 3 (1956–1957), 109–139.

Hooykaas, R., 'Science and Religion in the Seventeenth Century (Isaac Beeckman)', *Free University Quarterly* 1 (1950–1952), 169–183.

Jocelyn, H. D., and Setchell, B. P., *Regnier de Graaf on the Human Reproductive Organs*. Oxford, 1972.

Keuning, J., *Willem Jansz. Blaeu, a Biography*. Amsterdam, 1973.

Leeuwenhoek, A. van, *The Collected Letters*. 9 vols. so far. Amsterdam, 1939.

Rooseboom, M., *Microscopium*. Leiden, 1956.

Ruestov, E. G., *Physics at Seventeenth and Eighteenth Century Leiden: Philosophy and the New Science in the University*. The Hague, 1973.

Schierbeek, A., *Jan Swammerdam, His Life and Works*. Amsterdam, 1967. English edition of the Dutch edition of 1947.

Schierbeek, A., *Measuring the Invisible World, the Life and Works of Antoni van Leeuwenhoek*. London, New York, 1959. Concise English version of the Dutch book of 1950–1951.

Sirks, M. J., *Botany in the Netherlands*. Leiden, 1935.

Stevin, S., *The Principal Works*. 5 vols., Amsterdam, 1955–1966.

Trevor-Roper, H. R., 'The European Witch-craze of the Sixteenth and Seventeenth Centuries'. In *Religion, the Reformation and Social Change*. 2nd ed. London, etc., 1972), pp. 90–192. Deals with Wier, Bekker and many others.

Van Helder, A., 'The Historical Problem of the Invention of the Telescope', *History of Science* 13 (1975), 251–263.

Articles on Dutch scientists of our period can be found in the periodicals *Janus, Bijdragen tot de Geschiedenis der Geneeskunde* and *Scientiarum*

Historia, in different languages. In Dutch: *Tijdschrift voor de geschiedenis der Geneeskunde, Natuurwetenschappen, Wiskunde en Techniek* (succeeded in 1978 the periodical GEWINA)

II. SOME LITERATURE IN DUTCH AND OTHER LANGUAGES

A history of the Netherlands, illustrated, can be found in J. and A. Romein, *De lage landen bij de zee* (Utrecht, 1934, with later editions). The book of these authors, *Erflaters van onze beschaving* (Amsterdam, 1938–1940, with later editions), also translated into German, is a cultural history in the form of biographies of leading figures, among them Stevin, Spinoza, Huygens and Boerhaave. An older, still valuable, cultural history is C. Busken Huet, *Het land van Rembrandt* (Haarlem, 1882–1884).

Biographical and bibliographical data can be found in *Nieuw Nederlandsch Biographisch Woordenboek* (10 vols., 1911–1937) for the Northern, and in *Biographie nationale de Belgique* (since 1866) and *Nationaal Biographisch Woordenboek* (since 1964) for the Southern Netherlands. A short account of the new science can be found in E. J. Dijksterhuis, *Het wereldbeeld vernieuwd, van Copernicus tot Newton* (Arnhem, 1931); it anticipates his larger work of 1950.

Here follow some monographs:

Baasch, E., *Holländische Wirtschaftsgeschichte*. Jena, 1927.

Baumann, E. D., *Uit drie eeuwen Nederlandse geneeskunde*. Amsterdam, ca. 1950.

Baumann, E. D., *François de la Boë Sylvius*. Leiden, 1949.

Baumann, E. D., *Cornelis Bontekoe, de theedoctor*. Oosterbeek, 1949.

Bierens de Haan, D., *Bouwstoffen voor de geschiedenis der wis- en natuurkundige wetenschappen in de Nederlanden*. 2 vols. Amsterdam, 1878–1887. These are thirty-three articles first published in the *Verhandelingen Koninklijke Akademie van Wetenschappen*, afd Wis- en Natuurkunde (from 1874 on, continued till 1892).

Bosmans, H., Articles on Tacquet, Stevin, van Roomen, De Saint Vincent, van Ceulen, Nicolaas Pietersz, and others in *Isis, Mathesis, Annales Société Scientifique Bruxelles* and other periodicals between 1901 and 1928. Bibliography by A. Rome, *Isis* **12** (1929, 92–112), see also *Archives Intern. Histoire des Sciences* (N.S.) **3** (1950), 629–656.

Burger, C. P., 'Amsterdamsche rekenmeesters en zeevaartkundigen in de zestiende eeuw', Part III of *De Amsterdamsche Boekdrukkers en Uitgevers*. Amsterdam, 1926.

Coiter, Volcher, No. 18 of *Opuscula selecta neerlandicorum de arte medica*

(Amsterdam, 1955). These *Opuscula* present re-editions of several physicians of former years, e.g., No. 10 (1931): Bontius' *De medicina indorum*, with translation and introduction.

Dijksterhuis, E. J., *Simon Stevin*. 's Gravenhage, 1943.

Geer, P. van, 'Hugeniana geometrica', *Nieuw Archief voor Wiskunde*, 7–10 (1906–1912), twelve articles.

Gugel, K. F., *Johann Rudolph Glauber*. Würzburg, 1955.

Haas, K., 'Die mathematischen Arbeiten von Johann Hudde', *Centaurus* 4 (1956), 235–284. See also J. MacLean, *Scientiarum Historia* 13 (1971), 144–162.

Hofmann, J. E., *Frans van Schooten der Jüngere*. Wiesbaden, 1962.

Hooykaas, R., *Geschiedenis der natuurwetenschappen*. Utrecht, 1971, with titles of other publications of this author.

Houtzager, H. L., 'Willem Piso, pionier van de tropische geneeskunde', *Spiegel Historiael* 12 (1977), 390–393.

Hunger, F. W. T., *Charles de l'Ecluse, Carolus Clusius, Nederlandsch Kruidkundige, 1526–1609*. 2 vols. Den Haag, 1927, 1943.

Huygens, C., *Oeuvres complètes*. 22 vols. Den Haag, 1888–1952. See in connection with this edition, E. J. Dijksterhuis, *Christiaan Huygens*. Haarlem, 1951.

Jaeger, F. M., *Cornelis Drebbel en zijn tijdgenoten*. Groningen, 1932.

Keuning, J., *Petrus Plancius. Theoloog en Geograaf 1552–1622*. Amsterdam. 1946.

Korteweg, D. J., *Het bloeitijdperk der wiskundige wetenschappen in Nederland*. Amsterdam, 1894.

Lamers, A. J. H., *Hendrik van Deventer, Medicinae Doctor (1651–1724). Leven en werken*. Assen, 1946.

Lindeboom, G. A., *Geschiedenis van de medische wetenschap in Nederland*. Bussum, 1972.

Lindeboom, G. A., *Reinier de Graaf. Leven en werken*. Delft, 1973.

Roever, J. G. de, *Jan Adriaansz. Leeghwater*. Amsterdam, 1944.

Rooseboom, M., *Bijdrage tot de geschiedenis der instrumentmakerskunst in de Noordelijke Nederlanden tot omstreeks 1840*. Leiden, 1950.

Rogge, H. C., 'Nicolaas Tulp', *De Gids* 3 (1880), 77–125.

Sassen, *Geschiedenis van de wijsbegeerte in Nederland*. Amsterdam, 1959.

Schierbeek, A., *Jan Swammerdam. Zijn leven en werken*. Lochem, 1947.

Schierbeek, A., *Antoni van Leeuwenhoek. Zijn leven en werken*. Lochem, 1950–1951.

Smet, A. de 'Copernic et les Pays-Bas', *Janus* 60 (1973), 13–23.

Smit, P., 'Paul Hermann (1646–1695), ein Vertreter der niederländischen Botanik des 17. Jahrhunderts', *Wissenschaftliche Beiträge Universität Halle* (1969), 69–82.

Smeur, A. J. E. M., *De zestiende-eeuwse Nederlandse rekenboeken*. 's Graven-hage, 1960.

Spaander, J., *De erfenis van Leeghwater*. Amersfoort, 1950.

Spronsen, J. W. van, 'Glauber, grondlegger van chemische industrie', *Nederl. Chemische Industrie* **5** & **6** (March 1970).

Stoeder, W., *Geschiedenis der pharmacie in Nederland*. Amsterdam, 1891.

Stuldreher-Nienhuis, J., *Verboden paradyzen*. Arnhem, Amsterdam, 1952. This book contains reproductions from the work of Maria Sibylla Merian. Also a biography (Arnhem, 1945).

Tierie, G., *Cornelis Drebbel*. Amsterdam, 1932.

Vendorp, H., and Baas-Becking, L. G. M., *Hortus Academicus Lugduno-Batavus 1587–1937*. Haarlem, 1938.

Vollgraff, J. A., 'Leidsche hoogleeraren in de natuurkunde in de 16de, 17de en 18de eeuw', *Jaarboek Vereeniging Oud-Leiden* (1913), 167–196.

Vollgraff, J. A., A biography (in French) of C. Huygens in vol. XXII of the *Oeuvres complètes*. Den Haag, 1950.

Vries, T. de, *Baruch de Spinoza in Selbstzeugnis und Bilddokumenten*. Reinbek, 1970.

Vrijer, M. J. A. de, *Henricus Regius. Een 'Cartesiaansch' hoogleeraar aan de Utrechtsche Hoogeschool*. 's Gravenhage, 1917.

Vuys, J. G., 'Steno in Leiden', *Janus* **62** (1975) 157–168. See also *Niels Stensen*. Leiden, 1968.

Waard, C. de, *De uitvinding der verrekijkers*. Den Haag, 1906. See the article by A. van Helder, cited above.

INDEX

153

STUDIES IN THE HISTORY
OF MODERN SCIENCE

Editors:

ROBERT S. COHEN (Boston University)
ERWIN N. HIEBERT (Harvard University)
EVERETT I. MENDELSOHN (Harvard University)